THE GAME CHANGER FOR NATIONAL TRANSFORMATION

WALE ADEWUMI

Fireword Resources

Ibadan, Nigeria

08033750871, 07052751663

DEDICATION

Dedicated to Everyone in pursuit of a sane society – especially those from the struggling nations plagued by poor leadership

CONTENTS

ACKNOWLEDGMENTS

This book, like everything else I have created in my life, is the result of a huge team effort. I extend my deepest gratitude and thank to:

My wife, Esther Adewumi and my son, Emmanuel Adewumi for their unflinching support that offer me a most conducive environment to create this book.

Also on the list of those whom I owe my gratitude are Wale Adegoke for his time in editing the book over and over again. Kehinde Osineye for his support at every stage of creating a better world along with me, our ideals which is encapsulated in this book.

Also, thanks to my numerous friends and team at Game Changer project.

FOREWORD

Many books have been written on moving the nation forward. This book is different as it goes straight to the root of Nigeria's problem and will further serve as a template for every nation seeking for meaning. It is the roadmap to national greatness.

I have this to say. I have to confess that this is a brilliant work to help create extraordinary transformation in individual, corporate and national frontiers.

My personal interest in national issues has projected me to occupy several offices in the public sector and once as Nigeria Ambassador to Philippines. On this premise, I have always and will continue to give my full backing to projects that will assist my country move forward: this book is one of such.

The Game Changer for National Transformation shows us convincingly why we are where we are as a nation and the simple secrets that can move us forward are embedded from the first page to the last.

It is a well balanced book articulated to speak to all irrespective of religion, political affiliation, tribe or group.

In this book, you will learn a step-by-step process that can move you and those around you forward. The strategies discussed are so logical, inviting and beneficial to create breakthrough for those who want to transform their world seamlessly.

This is a book for leaders.

Sit back as you explore this life changing book.

Dr Yemi Faronmbi

A Statesman and former Ambassador to Philippines

Wale Adewumi

INTRODUCTION

Over the years diverse and several intervention programs had been designed by government, corporate organizations, religious bodies and individuals to bring changes and transformation into the nation. We need to appreciate those whose efforts are of sincere hearts and purposes.

Although we are yet to be where we ought to be, those efforts together had taken us so far. Without noble efforts as such, the nation would have been worse for it: lives have been preserved, civil wars checked and unrest nipped in the bud. If there be any reprieve or rest, it is for the sake of these relentless efforts.

We need to applaud the efforts of these men and women who so believe in the future of Nigeria above the general sentiments around them. On their shoulders rest the dawn of a new era, when the nation will rise majestically in prominence in the comity of nations as we become the center of a new world; with civilized culture, transformed laws, customs and values that uphold growth and development of our realms.

We should be humbled by those great efforts, many of which are not seen by many of us. Some did these at the backside, in hunger and wants believing and stretching, hoping and wanting for the days ahead when songs of comfort will break forth from every lip: I know some of them. In this labour, some have died, yet others remain strong and steady. Together, they are the heroes on the sidelines.

You may not be known or celebrated, but I can tell you, God holds you in high esteem as a repairer of breaches and a builder of nation. I say unequivocally, may God bless you as you keep labouring for a greater Nigeria.

My own effort is like one of those unknown heroes of our nation. For some two decades ago I have had the panting and desire to see my country, Nigeria become great in every sense. Ever since, I have been busy in one capacity or the other on the project Nigeria. But all my efforts were also from the minor.

In the year 2009, I conceptualized a thought of national rebirth and rebranding: "I AM THE CHANGE NIGERIA NEEDS", which has begun to gain momentum and recognition.

My belief is that the individuals have the power to bring changes to Nigeria. Clusters of individual efforts coming together build a nation.

Along the line a political party in Nigeria picked "Change" as their party slogan. Then I wanted to rest my oars but after a while, I realized that their concept of change was not exactly what I conceptualized, so my team began work again. This was year 2015 AD.

In the process of time, I saw a course program by The World Bank Group titled: Citizens Engagement, the Game Changer for Development? Going through the course program, I saw very much similarity to the concept of change designed in The Real Change Nigeria Needs project. Upon the completion of the course, my artefact and the sum of my project was scored to be among the best. The change project submission strongly pushed me to score distinction at the end of the course. The World Bank Group assessors recommended that the model be translated into a national intervention program, and a particular assessor believed that its usefulness could serve as a template for nations in quest of meaningful transform.

The same concept is hitherto elaborated into a book to serve the needs of hundreds, thousands and millions who might be looking for a model upon which to build a transformation ideology.

I want to believe that this book will serve you and will be of vital usefulness as you become the change the world needs.

You are the change!

The slide version of the artifact can be viewed at this link:

http://www.slideshare.net/fireword/final-project-sustainable-change

coursera.org

MARCH 16, 2016

Statement of Accomplishment

WITH DISTINCTION

ADEWUMI SAMSON ADEWALE

HAS SUCCESSFULLY COMPLETED THE WORLD BANK GROUP'S MOOC ON

Engaging Citizens: A Game Changer for Development?

Government works best when citizens are directly engaged as stakeholders. This course provides an overview of citizen engagement, critical analyzing of how it can be leveraged most effectively to achieve development outcomes.

JEFF THINDWA
PRACTICE MANAGER, OPEN AND COLLABORATIVE
GOVERNANCE, THE WORLD BANK

BJÖRN-SÖREN GIGLER
SENIOR GOVERNANCE SPECIALIST , THE WORLD BANK

TIAGO PEIXOTO
TEAM LEAD, GOVERNANCE GLOBAL PRACTICE , THE
WORLD BANK

HELENE GRANDVOINNET
GOVERNANCE EXPERT, GLOBAL GOVERNANCE
PRACTICE IN THE AFRICA REGION

Chapter One

THE CHANGE NIGERIA NEEDS

Somebody told me: "We do not want a political change; the Nigerian people need a real life transforming change!"

In the same vein, this book is not a treatise prepared to eulogize any single person, entity or political party. It is prepared with the aim of eliciting an inclusive form in which you become the major player. It is written to prepare you for the great assignment which only you can carry out in the making of the new Nigeria which we all desire.

The nation, Nigeria is on a cross road, the leadership and citizens together are confused and lost as to what next to do to bring about succor to the people. The leaders are confused, so the people. We have tried several and diverse strategies all to no avail: policies have been formulated, rules made, projects executed, ideologies shared and policies implemented yet without achieving much respite.

The truth is evident in this: taking over the rein of governance from the colonial master has not made our lots better. The relics are out there to prove the point.

Hindsight

When the colonial masters rule their citizens back in their native land, they rule with different strategies, principles and mindset. But to us, they sold inverted principles, strategies and mindset that made us fight, squabble and get ourselves corrupted on nothingness. They gave us a farce version of "government".

The government becomes the little god we were all called to serve (government is a figment of imagination which takes its strength from whatever we imagined it to be).

The bigger we make the government, the weaker the society becomes. The much we depend on the government the more retrogressive we will become. This is why Nigeria and many of the colonized nations are where they are today - we depend overly on the government!

If we believe we have to wait on the government for virtually everything, we are likely not going to succeed or make much meaning out of life.

Deliberately or not we have been programmed to think in a certain way. Our creative power has been taken away. Our resilience and strength to strive have been subordinated at the altar of government. When you think someone else is there to carry your burden, you cripple the development of your own capability over time.

As long as we make the government the little god that sees to our welfare, determines our fate and solves most of our life's problems we are in trouble.

I am not talking about the government being the problem; instead, I am talking about the perception and imagery of government and governance.

The perception of a shadow and the image itself are two different things. If we are frightened out of proportion, we can make a ghost out of a shadow. In reality a shadow is not synonymous to a ghost (perception issue). The perception of government and governance in Nigeria has contributed to why we are where we are today.

Government is neither good nor bad; it is what we make out of it that is important.

The Denomination

The denomination of a good government is this: the empowerment of the people.

The purpose of a government is to empower the people to become more; helping them to realize the best use of their potentials, to help the individual citizen look to self as the answer.

True government should not sap the people or reduce them in any way.

The government should enhance and not adapt the people.

To enhance is to help them become more, achieve more and gain more of what they could become or realize; providing an enabling environment to display their creative ability, talents, gifts and entrepreneurial ability and whatever they possess.

To adapt the people is to convert the people for a different use. This is about abusing the people, taking away their desire, dreams and aspirations because of imposed limitations. At the end, the people turn out to become an inferior personality of their real being.

Backward nations take power from the people and end up adapting them for lesser cause. Weak leaders believe that when you empower the followers, you end up losing them. This is what I call stinking thinking.

A corrupt government takes that which belongs to others; at the expense of the society and uses it for their own ego.

Also, a society that places the weak to rule over the strong is a perverted one; this is an adaptation of the trained hands and those with leadership ability to be subjected to the level of mediocre. As the day is far away from the night, any society that favours the weak at the expense of the strong can never know progress, advancement and greatness. In such situations, the strong is repressed and adapted or fashioned to act below their innate endowments while the weak that is promoted right in his weak state is denied the process of true growth and the satisfaction that comes from achieving what is truly ones due.

A child who gets everything free without his own input often abuse things and the good life itself. The more you pamper a child, the more you lose him. Expose him, let him fight his own battles and he will live to appreciate life. A nation, people, tribe and individuals who live for free things will never realize their true potentials. Just as a spoilt child is menacing, indulging and destructive so is a spoilt individuals who get things they do not labour for or things they do not deserve.

Give people the rights to earn their due and peace will be restored to our land. Injustice, inequalities, and non-equity are together troubling gangrene that is eating health out of nationhood.

A spoilt child will destroy others and finally destroy himself. Children who did not earn their worth often fritters it away through frivolity: bad relationships, waste and addiction. Of what use then is helping a child to destroy himself? In the same way, when we steal from one tribe or group to help a weakling to cover-up a facade of federation, we are only helping to destroy what we tend to pamper. Time to think deeply: there is nothing really free except what will end up gagging a man's capability of a truly rich life.

Match opportunities with growth; create a level playing field as each is helped to become better. Let the citizens find their joy and satisfaction not in things but in the very process of becoming, sacrificing and giving.

A true government is positioned to empower its citizens to realize their potentials and to find meaning to their own lives through active contribution to the well being of the world they belong.

The Root

The colonial master when they were about leaving called for a referendum. They designed what government should be; we did not design the government system we are operating. It was handed over to us and we never questioned the content because the so called government was made to favour the center and the few fortunate ones. It is a government that allows greed and corruption to thrive. The clamour has remained: whosoever gets to the center controls the power, resources and the people. Because of this, the vast of African nations and the colonized worlds have not known rest, respite or progress. Ours has been a land for savages. The problem in the actual sense is not the people but the model of governance we are using.

Anyone who gets to the center would never be able to effect any meaningful change until we overhaul the present form of government. This will continue until we have strong leaders who would question such system of government and this will require sincere and selfless personalities.

When a government becomes too strong, it weakens its constituency. When much power is reposed in a government, it adapts most of its citizens into herds of communities; and everyone begins to think that his life depends on the central power. When much resources is taken to the center, it automatically create an unmatched grandeur and opulence for those who are fortunate to be at the center; thus making them assume the position of little gods to be worshiped. While those who are outside the corridor of power will go through any length of Machiavellian intrigues to be in power.

The name or type of government being practiced does not matter, what really matters is the content, fruit and dividend of governance. Most of the colonized world including Nigeria may adopt federalism, confederalism or democratic system but they have not been able to undo the subtle system beneath our government system.   The strength of a structure is firmly attached to its foundation.

Until the foundation is visited and addressed, no change of worth can be achieved.

The Pot of Death

There is a stolen mandate that has taken away sleep from all of us and we are all awake by the same dilemma. The man in opulence could not sleep because of the marauder. The marauder in turn has no rest because he is hungry, for the man in opulence has taken over his inheritance. Sleep has been murdered, and to rest for both, there must be a middle ground for settlement!

To get the point home I will take a moment to tell us a very good story I heard when I was young. It is not about how true it was but the lesson it scored.

This is the story.

Once, there were three good friends. They had been together for years, no one ever heard of their quarrel, and if there was ever any quarrel, they amicably settled issues among themselves. Their status difference was nothing to them as they were all contented hunters and farmers. They took turn in one another home and had many things in common except their wives of course.

When they did not go to their respective farms they do go on hunting expedition together. In one of such hunting expedition, they had hardly gone far into the forest when a man ran past them like someone who was frightened as he kept shouting: Death! Death! Death!

Hunters in the olden days were trained to be bold and fearless; these three friends looked into one another's eyes and agreed to move in the direction where the unknown man ran away from. They courageous inched forward and on the alert.

Almost the same time, they saw at a distance some brilliant bars beneath a tree. They gasped and prayed it should be real. They all rushed forward, felt the bars and smelled them. They lived in an age that used gold, so they agreed these must be real gold.

To be sure they are not being careless, they went ahead a little for more search but could not find anything that represented death or danger. They came back to the tree and were happy about their new prospect of riches.

As they gazed on the large bars of gold, each of them began to imagine how to take ownership of the gold all alone. One of them went to town to buy wine to celebrate their fortune and he had it poisoned along the way. When he came, the other two shot him dead, and they drank the wine only to die from the effect of the poison. They all died around the pot of gold.

Our system of government is the pot of gold that is leading to the death and destruction of countless numbers. Take the pot of gold away and we will begin to live together in peace, love and harmony. The pot of gold has divided us along the line of religion, social stratification, beliefs, ideologies, and ethnicity. Each constituent or group wants to poison or destroy the other to get things closer to its own side. This has led to death, poverty, corruption and conflicts. The negative impact is growing day by day.

Free or unearned riches are death, the more surplus the more adversarial such becomes.

How the Angel of Death was Reared

Government has become a lucrative power house where the greatest robbery has been instituted to steal from the people. The government should be for the people but in our case, it is the reverse whereby the people are to serve the government; a service that deify the government and the holders of power. It is noteworthy to consider this: no one will know rest when things are run in disorderly manner.

The upsurge of Boko Haram menace in Nigeria is a reflection of what we are saying. It might seem to have started on the wing of religious extremism but a closer look revealed a people seeking for expression and recognition. They only create a camouflage through the religions platform. The leaders of Boko Haram have seen the picture of grandeur, wealth and power accorded to the central government, so they wanted a taste of that even though in a crude way; this was why they strived to carve out a caliphate of their own. To their followers, they gave a bloated picture of religious hopes but the inner circle knows it is a thirst for power and control. This is how you come to know the genuineness of their leaders: How many of the leaders ever take the task of voluntary suicide bombing expeditions? Thousands have died in the wake of the bedeviled giant called Boko Haram.

We need to remember that Boko Haram has politicians who sponsor their notoriety. It was said that some of their kingpins were once thugs of the rich politicians.

Not to go too far. In the South-South region of Nigeria we do have knowledge of how militancy was reared.

Some camps of politicians were jostling for the central control of governorship seat while the incumbent fought to retain the office and other contenders also fight dirty to take over. Each group went forth to fortify themselves by recruiting, training and equipping their mercenaries of death. It was thirst for power and control that gave life to the angel of death called militancy.

The list continues of the ills that non-serendipitously crept in from the government and style of governance.

The Problem is in Flow

In Third World nations, the leadership is designed in such a way to create control, to accumulate resources to the center, wanting to hold on in a way that everyone is placed at the mercy of government. The resources of the third world and the advanced nations is not much of a difference; the difference is in the distribution or what I call flow. The health of a nation is the ability to create a flow of resources and benefits in a just and fair manner.

When a river is stopped and dammed, it begins to gather volume and weight until it grows into a massive and impressive proportion. It gets to a volume size that it becomes dangerous to the neighbourhood. This is how large and impressive our leadership system looked like, large and impressive but dangerous to the society.

Whenever a river keeps its flow, it serves much useful purposes. It creates more life around it. A flowing river may look lean compared to the dammed one but at the end, it serves much useful purposes.

We need to keep a lean government and make it less attractive by creating a new kind of attraction. We need to change the rule of play in a way that it will attract more participation from the citizens. We need to device means of sharing and distribution in the spirit of fairness and equity. We need to get things done by the right person and get certain and equitable dividends across to the right person. A contented man in his own world is not easily enticed by hazardous adventure of militancy or terrorism no matter the fortune entailed. I have come to know that the average man is easily satisfied once his basic needs are met.

Terrorism is spawned by poverty and imbalances.

Take away frustration from your people, give them their land, and give them their place and what is due to them. This is what the average man will always demand: enough to live by and power to express self when there is need. This should be the soul of governance and when this is done; loyalty and patriotism to national cause soar higher while retrogressive and vicious acts will be minimized.

When the people are well catered for, their interest brought to the fore and are empowered to be more and to do more, a nation rears up to become optimized for productivity with far greater output than the initial invested input. Once there is a flow, most conflicts and agitation will naturally subside.

Taking Closer Look at the Root Cause:

There is always cause to an effect. When certain things fail and are not working, there is underlying causes. Nigeria project has not been working; and to put it on the progressive lane, we must find out the foundational problem.

The real problem with Nigeria is not the citizens or the leaders per se; though for ages each side of the divide has been pointing accusing finger to the other. The problem with Nigeria is in its foundation.

Have we not wondered that thousands of new leaders emerge during every new election years? Those new leaders were once normal average citizens but when they get to the center, they are swallowed by the system; like the mysterious Bermuda Triangle. So our ill fated leadership experimentation has continued till date without yielding expected dividend for growth and a sustained change.

This is the evil of the colonial masters: they put too much of power and resources to the central government. The stronger ones fight to take it and the rest who could not get to the corridor of power look helplessly waiting for the crumbs that fall down from the table of opulence. This evil is further entrenched and made us think we cannot change for better.

We have come to term that government is unquestionable and cannot be held accountable – above board and above the law. We have come to think that citizens are pawns to nourish the existence of government and those who hold the rule.

We became independent as a nation bodily but our souls are still enslaved to the pattern of government used to govern the colonized nations.

The colonial masters have a different system for ruling their subjects back in their native land and another yardstick of government in their colony.

In their native land, the government is positioned to serve the people, to satisfy their interests, well-being and advancement. The leaders see the people in their native land as their own citizens and are respected, ensuring that their self-esteem is preserved. Citizens of the colonial masters are protected in any part of the world. In return, the citizens are ready to give back whatever they have to preserve and move forward their common interest. Thus, this fulfills the law of give and take.

Down in their colony, the colonial masters do not go there to serve but to plunder. They colonized nations to usurp power and take advantage of the weak nations. The sole purpose of colonization is trade and exploitation. Thus the people in the colony are seen as errand boys, servants and the low class; the inferior people. The colonial masters see themselves as the superior race (the elevated citizen of the world) that must be worshiped.

In order to perpetuate their dominance, they apply force and cruelty. Goods and resources are moved from the people's domain back to their central government in their home country leaving the nations they governed impoverished. The expression of their governance clearly shows that they are not out in the interest of the people of the colony; instead the people are seen as tools to sustain the government of the colonial masters.

This was the kind of government handed over to Nigeria in 1960. What changed was the skin colour of the leaders in government, the white man is gone, the black man turns in but the heart is the same. We kept doing things the same old way: for the art and objective of governance remain the same; to plunder.

A son who all his life watched his father bully his mom may not know any other way of handling a woman. If he does not undergo a personal rebirth or reorientation, when he gets married, he will think that the only way to win a woman's submission is being high handed.

The first generation leaders were tutored about the art of governance by the colonial masters. Through observation they learned so much from the white men. When the masters were gone, they took turn to loot, exploit and steal from the people. They saw the white man taking advantage of the vulnerability of the citizens, so they learn to do the same. The new leaders after 1960 see themselves as the new "white" who must be served and not to serve. It has become seemingly incurable syndrome growing in magnitude by the day.

The average kid today sees leadership in any sphere or sector of the nation as an opportunity to loot and enrich oneself. To further grow the expanse of greed, we keep making the center of leadership attractive with "unlimited" opportunity to wealth and power that it becomes easy to miss the mark of leadership as a call to serve.

Going this way, we will never get it right. It is time to make the needed shift from aristocratic style of government leadership to people centered leadership.

It is time to unfold a new kind of change – The sustainable positive type!

Chapter Two

THE EFFECT

When water is poisoned at source it will also have the traces of the poison wherever it flows.

What we were handed as a government was a tainted one. Upon this, most governance and leadership were patterned after. Check every tier of government and every sector. We have leaders and people who are there thinking of what they could make out of the system.

The colonial master's primary goal is about how best they could harness their colony with the intent of maximum exploitation. The leaders they breed follow suit.

At the federal level we have been able to raise many presidents who thought the resources of the nation are theirs and to be used as they wish. Many of them successfully diverted huge sum of money for personal gains. To make it worse, they stole their people's money to help the already settled economy of the advanced nations through diverse money laundering tactics. It was a case of an ex Head-of-State whose loots have to be expatriated over and over from different offshore accounts.

This implies that such leaders do not have their people's interest in their heart in the first place. The citizens committed to their care do not matter to them. The programs that see the light of the day are those that have direct benefits to them or the cause they have vested interest in. They are vestiges of the colonial masters.

In the same vein, other national leaders take after the overall head. They share and plunder what rightly belongs to the populace: the colonial master's style of governance. Everybody is looking for the opportunity to plunder and take advantage of the other. We think in terms of "my own" and not "our own". There is no cohesive force of corporate drive for a common laurel and achievement. Each person, every tribe and religion want to outshine without thinking of his fellow's well being. This is the debased mind sold to us and which we kept on propagating. If we keep nourishing our debased mind of personal gain and aggrandizement at the expense of others, we should not expect so much from the system.

We could see the expression of our inordinate propensity for self in diverse ways and forms.

Example of the Lawmakers

Taking a look at the senate, the federal representatives and the State House of Assemblies one would notice that many of the bills passed in one way or the other do not represent the interest of the masses. Often those bills were created to protect or benefit a specific class.

The said lawmakers may want to argue that they are doing great; to these ones I say: talk is cheap - by their fruit you shall know them. No matter the line of defense, it is clear that the common man is not well favoured by most of the bills rolled out.

Nigeria is a wonderland where the laws hardly affect the super rich and powerful; they always have a way out. Don't we wonder about the porosity of the Nigerian laws which seldom affect the high class, the rich, the nobles and the politicians? There was a case of a Nigerian leader who was acquitted by Nigerian law, but the same man was charged and imprisoned in a foreign country on the same charges.

Our laws are deliberately designed that way to protect the big guys at the expense of the rest.

Why do you think we have more bills protecting the larger corporations, rich individuals and the powerful? This happens when lawmakers are after personal gains: bribes corrupt good judgment. The conglomerates, multinationals and large firms have a way of paying dues to favour bills that will protect them: even when they are over charging or offering inferior services.

Many of the accursed bills are purported to stifle the growth of the common man, but in a subtle way. I believed that many of our regulatory agencies and controlling agencies are often paid hugely by some mega corporate firm to trample the upcoming under the guise of regulation. These nasty deals are done under the cover of this ill intentioned bills and laws.

Many of the bills and laws around us do not empower the common man; until the common man is empowered the economy will never be liberated. Empowered people build an empowered nation!

Good laws will create enabling environment and equal opportunity for all. But in a corrupt society some people are placed above the law because some powerful lawmakers are induced to tamper with the laws and constitution in a negative way. Somebody may not like what I am saying here, but clearly no name is called; what we want if you are affected is that you choose to make a change now.

The lawmakers were placed or elected there by the people and for the people but they never saw it that way. Once they get there the negative mindset goes to work: the evil model from the colonial masters that represent its own interest by lording it over its subjects.

It was a sorry expression of a man's faculty to call his subject apes. This was the picture of a colonial master of his colony – he sees them as not better than apes (animals) to be used for personal own end. This therefore portends the colonial masters as bad leaders.

In their footstep we have raised from our own kindred worst leaders bedeviled with reckless pursuit of personal interests.

Examples of the Governors

Coming downward, we have governors of states who believe the state is their personal possession. They give the expression as if they own the people and whatever magnanimity they do is of personal benevolence. It is a common thing for a governor to come on air to blah what he has done as if he used his personal funds to execute projects. Their expression shows that they do not think deep that whatever they do are of duty of theirs, a mandate and rights of the people. Many of these governors go offshore to borrow loans which would put the future generations into bondage.

Why do most of them borrow in the first place? When they borrow, they have access to large fund, with large fund opportunity to "execute project", to execute project is to gain opportunity to pocket some of these large sum in percentages. Self enriching at the expense of the people!

The colonial masters seem better in this wise: even though they came to pillage our resources, they left behind durable projects, structures and work. But our own native leaders who are of the same blood are demonically possessed with greed as they loot our common good to the skin.

Things are falling apart because of the height of greed and self centeredness of our leaders; everything falls from the center and decays from the foundation. The whole lot is excited into the race of greed and self.

Nigerian politicians are mostly of the same bunch which includes the lower cadres and tiers: the local government chairmen, political advisers, federal ministers and commissioners. Everyone seems to look for opportunity for personal enrichment.

A Problem Rooted in All of Us

Now to us: many times we are often too quick to point at the leaders as the woe of our dear nation. But looking critically we discovered that the problem of Nigeria is not really a leadership problem but a system failure: using the wrong blueprints to run our affairs; a blueprint that originated with a colonial system of administration.

If it were a leadership problem, Nigeria would by now be settled, re-engineered and healed. All the first generation leaders after the nation's independence from Britain are all dead. Many of the second generation leaders are already leaving the scene, yet leadership is getting worst by the day. The problem is that emerging leaders are getting indoctrinated after the former leader's blueprint: the blueprint that makes the citizens second class and tools to nourish the upper class. A template of governance that makes the citizens answerable to the leaders and not the other way round, a system that makes servants out of the citizens.

As we were saying, the old breeds of leaders are gone, but where do the new breeds of leaders emerged from? They emerged right from our midst.

This implies that Nigeria problem is rooted in all of us!

Here are some instances: going to a government organization, gate-men who are one of the first contacts in an establishment are often known to be notorious for asking for tips from visitors. The office assistant will not allow one to see his boss until you tip him and the files of proposals may become missing until the director knows what is in it for him. Permanent secretary connives with politicians in power to divert or loot the treasury. There is no end to the whims and caprices of civil servants to extort or divert funds. The problem of Nigeria is neither that of politicians nor that of civil servants alone; every sector has its own share.

Taking a look at the religious circle, many of our religious leaders are self-serving from the lowest to the highest echelon. They cash on the vulnerability of their followers to build up their own financial empires using gimmicks and falsehood.

To avoid sounding absolute here about wealth; wealth is good but should not be built at the expense of others.

A man who creates value for others has the right to be rich. It is a good thing to be rich while we bring solution to our world, but it becomes evil when we try to become rich by making life difficult for others through subversive means. A Bill Gates wealth is the right kind, a robber's wealth is the wrong kind because no value is exchanged for the wealth gotten.

I have heard of terrible stories of policemen ransacking dead accident victims to collect money and valuables. Should we go so bad and reckless in our quest for personal gain?

Our security personnel depending on the power of the gun would often use violence and force to have their ways. Altogether, they have forgotten that they are there for the rest citizens and for a time.

The cabman who takes advantage of his passenger is not different. Give him bigger responsibility he will act in the same way; in the spirit of lording it over others.

Many lecturers would do anything possible to sleep with the female students under their tutelage and they would intimidate any male student who trespasses around their female choices. This act has led to many students being failed or withdrawn from schools. Instead of using their position for the good of mankind, they utilize it as means for taking advantage of others. In the same token, they extort others through unjustified sales of lecture materials. This is a group of enlightened calibre from whom much is expected.

I remembered one of my lecturers, an old man who stooped so low that he would have wanted me expelled from the university. He would, if he had his way, get me bundled with cultists. His problem was that a female friend whom he was interested in moved him to envy, he thought in his heart that I was her lover. This was a mere assumption which could have cost an innocent person his education.

The traders and business men also have a way of short-changing the people. Their greed is one of the drivers of inflation in our society. A little fluctuation in the chain of demand and supply often reflect in pricing, this tells why prices may never be stabilized relatively for a long time. In Nigeria, most prices that go up seldom come down because our price increase is a bandwagon type. The following has been noted centrally as influencing pricing significantly in this part of the world: salary increment, fuel price and exchange rate. These three factors are strong indices all over the world, but there should be proportionality and justification. In Nigeria, most price action is outrageous and reflecting our mind set to take advantage of situations.

Labour groups, unions and associations have become another terrible sector. In every sense of bargaining, each side should have what to bring to the table for mutual benefit. The existence of labour groups has been serving a lopsided benefits which are about bargains for increase in salary and benefits. The other side of bargains which relate to standardization of output and productivity is often overlooked. You cannot get something with nothing to give in exchange; without equitable exchange there will be collapse of a system, it is just a matter of time. We have corporations closed down because of the insensitivity of the labour group to justify salary increase with productivity.

The economy of any nation is a reflection of the type of labour group that exist within it: consumption oriented or production oriented. The roles of the labour group in revamping an economy cannot be over-emphasized. We can easily tell what kind of labour groups we have in the nation by the health of the economy.

Zeroing upon the labour groups leaders, we have also seen on the increase their self-serving tendency. They do not bargain in the interest of their followers most of the time. Instead they subvert their followers to achieve their own sinister gains; they cunningly wrestle for gains from the employers and the government by employing hundreds and thousands of naïve followers through strike actions.

We need honest and sincere labour group leaders to advance the nation; I mean labour leaders that empower their followers and not their own greed.

The list would go on without restrain: Every sector, group and individual has in one way or the other contributed to where we are presently as a nation. The sum of the individual component makes up the whole; to absolve you of all responsibility makes you shallow, irresponsible and ordinary. Take up responsibility and make your sphere of contact much better than you met it. It is time you truly live.

Most of us are often too quick to point an accusing finger to the government, politicians and leaders as our problems for underdevelopment. But we should begin to think in a balanced way that the leaders emerge from within us and that whatever dominant characters and vices they display are reflection of the whole.

If we all make up our minds to do things right, become considerate and begin to serve a cause that is beyond us, things will change. Let us take our eyes away from what others have to do but looking inward to what we have to offer. Whatever we want from others starts from us.

Chapter Three

START THE BOOMERANG

Whatever you want done must start with you!

No empire is built without the man with the vision in the center of it. Somebody must be available to drive the desired change. You have to activate whatever you so eagerly desire.

The Lessons from a Beggar

Even the beggar knows how to start his own kind of boomerang, though not the healthy kind in most cases. He takes his seat strategically, brings out his beggar's plate, yet he will not let it be empty throughout if he wants to make enough cash for the day and he will also not let it be filled up before bagging it. Nobody will want to put more money into a beggar's plate that is already full; not even me. In the same way, an empty plate does not motivate giving. So to start his begging for the day, the beggar often drops the first few coins from his own purse into the plate. The few coins say a lot:

People don't want to be seen as being bad and the conscience has a way of helping in this regard. 'If somebody can give to this beggar, I should also', the mind will often play on us.

The man who starts a good cause is speaking approval or condemnation to the heart of others. Doing the right thing strengthens and emboldens others to act in the same manner. Deep within everyone is the innate capacity and desire to be good. Start the change work and you will be amazed at the large number of people that will form bee line behind, identifying with you. It is about starting.

The beggar drops the first few coins to attract more alms. You must make the first sacrifice. People want to see how serious you are about a vision, your sacrifice will speak volume about your intentions. Whatever you are not willing to give to, you cannot affect. When you have a stake in a thing people respect and identify with you.

Don't just talk about the problems of the nation; take up the responsibility for certain area you think you can affect. People who complain are plain talkers. He who is busy offering solutions would rarely have time to deal with unimportant issues.

Shift base, change position and become a change maker in your own world!

The beggar's initial few coins soon begin to attract other coins and it becomes a large sum, large impressive sum.

To appear empty and without value is to be treated as without value. To poise as nobody, is to be nobody. If you think you don't have, you cannot have. If you think you are an ordinary citizen you will be treated as such. If you think you don't have a voice your voice will never matter where it matters.

You are what you think and you are what you do!

Put your few coins forward and let it begin to attract other coins. If your desire is to build and live within the walls of a great nation then begin to do things that are relevant to bringing change as you would desire it. In so doing you are building up yourself into an authority. When you start, it may look like a few coin, a little unattractive gestures, a little principled stand for what is right, a little service, giving of yourself or sacrifice. It is a matter of time, it will grow in momentum.

The world would always see things in two distinct shades: of negative or positive. No matter the false image of opulence we may create for ourselves, the world will always give back to us what we sow into it. If you create chaos in your trail, distort the truth and take that which belongs to others, it is a matter of time before you see all that you build with ill gotten wealth crumble before your own eyes, then you will stand where I stand now: You will recognize the wisdom of character as weighing better than riches and a good name being better than silver and gold. The man who creates negative effect will no doubt harvest abundant of same in due season.

Often, people who have equal or surpassing tendency for evil complain more about the societal outlook. My mom used to tell me: "It takes a proud person to know another proud person." In a simple language: the world you live in is a reflection of you.

When you choose to do the right thing, right people begin to increase around you; situations begin to take on new light. When you choose to live right, you will begin to populate the right people and situation around you. For the advancing man, all things around him begin to advance.

The Mob Advantage

Another lesson from the beggar's plate is this: people give to what people give to, people will go to where others go and people will do what others do. We live in a bandwagon society whether in the religion circle or political setting. People don't always ask themselves why they do what they do. Most people are wired in a way that they just do and act in a way that conforms to the popularly accepted action, lifestyle or way of life around them.

There was this story of people running and scampering for places to hide their heads. This happened at Oshodi-Oke in Lagos. A stranger came down from a vehicle to the confusion; but before he began to run he took courage to ask a man running towards him what the problem was.

The man replied in Pidgin English breathing heavily: "I no know, I see people de run me too com de run."

The above just summed up the fact that we often do things without asking questions but because others are doing the same.

The villainous political juggernauts are master strategists that make good use of the mobilization technique to win the heart of the people even against their wishes. You may wonder how the religious lords of the Jews sank the voice of the multitudes that were singing Hosanna few days earlier. And they nailed Jesus publicly, before these same multitudes. Within few days the multitudes shifted from Jesus to the Pharisees.

Nigeria has a long history of corrupt leaders governing her. Today, these same leaders still retain followers in their millions in spite of overwhelming evidence of their crimes and looting. How do they achieve such feat? The fleeced and impoverished citizens are still the one ganging up to protect the wicked leaders.

Sometime ago, a high profile Nigerian (referenced earlier in this book) was released from jail in a foreign country upon completing his jail term. He was jailed abroad for corruption related charges but prior to this time, his country judges had acquitted him of all corrupt charges leveled against him. Although his country knew why he was jailed, they knew the extent to which he plundered yet they came out to celebrate him ostensibly. Their argument was based on a groundless reason: that corruption was everywhere. The same people protect the same corrupt leaders and at the same time go out lampooning the state of our national deterioration. Corruption will be with us to the extent at which we tolerate it.

Back to issue: Without raising questions, average people will follow leaders that other people follow without questioning their rationale. The average man thinks like a herd of cattle. The herd nature is a good attribute if it serves in achieving good and fair governance. Cooperation should be achieved when it tends toward advancement of all. But we need to be like a lion when we are being led to our destruction. We need to be bold, ask questions and take charge – appropriately.

In the developing world like ours, the herd nature of man is a tendency that causes them to be raised as a mob. The word mob is the root word for mobilization. To mobilize is to devise a strategy that absorbs the very first few collaboration starting with you; in no time it grows in number and quantum.

To raise a mob, the bad leader who often has influence or money or both would go out and create propaganda, some sort of sentiments or bias which he pushes forth to his first adopters. Propaganda, sentiments and biases are diversionary tool of wicked or weak leaders.

The sentiments include religion, tribal or class based in order to divide the people and win some of them.

If people would identify with a bad leader on sentiment of religion, tribe or class they will also identify with your cause if you build it around the people's interests. One principal interest of mankind is their economic well being, yet with good communication you can still mobilize many to your cause with little or no money but with some other forms of gains.

You need to learn to mobilize for people and fund. People go where people go, so money goes to where money goes. You need money and you need people; but it is you that must set the system in motion. Again, in a situation where it is difficult to sell them based on the power of money, you must be able to sell them a vision of a great and expanded future for your team and the society. You must be able to paint a desirable future of freedom and prosperity. Many of us buy into the rich picture of God's paradise. I know you do, and you will want to do all you can to be there.

God himself sold us a fair deal of a resplendent beautiful future with him if we live right as mortal and hell waits if we live contrary. This is what we were told and many of us bought into the deal.

Many people will go all the way and endure whatever form of hardship if you could offer them a fair haven at the end of the struggles.

Paint the beautiful picture your vision is set to achieve and you will not find it too difficult to kick-start and get the people to your side;

the premise of your picture is the solution you intend bringing to the world.

The Shine, the Life

Always remember that your life is a solution offered to a hurting world. If all problems of the world are already solved there would be no need of you being here on earth. Every creation is an answer for another creation: this is why people who live for their own personal gains are to be seen as being short-sighted.

The full strength of someone is to serve others just as the full strength of the sun is positioned to serve billions of creations. As the sun shines, it gives life to billions of living creations.

Also, be ready to be used up for the cause of others like the sun. The sun is used up for the rest of creations. As it burns, it is being consumed just as the candle burns to give light and in the process used up. The sun is like the big candle. As the candle burns it is being used up to supply light around. The sun is likewise burning to create energy for other creations.

Be used up for others; this is when you have truly lived. It is only in being spent for others that the society grows, expands and advances. It is anathema to growth when everyone chose to live for personal goals: living for oneself is a sure way to kill a society.

Think of its impact on the rest of the world if the sun will take away its shine. Within twenty-four hours billions of lives will be lost. Think of a world without the moon, the stars, air and water?

The animals and plants all have their places. Looking at it from a distance you will want to conclude that a goat lives for itself but at a closer look, you will see that it balances the ecosystem and food-chain at certain point.

You bring balance to the world system if you choose to see it as such. You are to make a difference and make the world around you a better place. Why are you here and what impact are you casting upon your neighbourhood and community? How do you discharge your duty?

Do you help people or oppress them? Are you out there to use people or help them to become better?

The change starts with you. Loosen up; allow the paradigm shift from the old self-serving mentality to others-centered mentality. In serving others you come face to face with your real self, this is the time you begin to exude the divine energy to express more of yourself; and it is the beginning of your walk into the hall of greatness.

It is a false life to live for self; driven by greed and vain pursuit. To burn for self without anyone walking in your light or benefitting from your living is to have lived a wasted life of emptiness.

When you wake up, what is your main preoccupation: To go help solve the world's problem or to go make a living for yourself? Making a living may be okay by you but that is what the average people out there do, and that is how far they go. To live large is to be extended to other people's cause.

Two people could be on the same job yet run their affairs on divergent principles. The one who stepped out to use his job as a platform to help others will be radiant, poised and confident of the unfolding life before him. While the man who had taken a job for a living will do all he could to get all he can and to can all he gets; and such people don't give back to the society. They have the entitlement syndrome whereby everything and everyone has to pay them one way or the other. In order to get more and enough, some go further becoming villains, scoundrels and cheats.

Most of those we call leaders in Nigeria are people who run after things; material acquisition. They turn every opportunity to means of making a living.

I am not saying earning income is bad, but to earn an income is only an integral part of living not an end. The end of living should be to affect the lives around you positively.

Exceeding Your Inputs

By keen observations, our Nigerian leaders most often think of what to get; this dirty flaw has smeared the souls of many. If we borrow money from The World Bank, do we put it into projects and infrastructure development which output will exceed the loan input? Unfortunately, these prodigal leaders will wine and dine with loaned funds and impoverished their citizens the more. They think of getting and not giving, by so doing leave no legacy behind.

Now back to you, indeed, to earn income should be a derivative of useful value delivered or service provided. I mean income should be as a result of giving out values in exchange for earnings. It predisposes that you should always think of giving ahead of getting and giving ahead of making your living indeed.

Give and you shall receive. Use your job, career, political office, business and any platform you may have as an opportunity to give. To learn to give is to learn to be contented, satisfied and be at peace. To grapple and grasp is to subject one's life to the misery of discontentment and loss of quietness of soul. If every employee cultivates the habit of giving and justified value in order to earn a specific income, we will have thriving businesses and organizations. A thriving organization will continue to have need of more employees which means increasing jobs and this will foster a healthy economy. Unfortunately many out there want to take advantage of their employers. This is not a good spirit if you really want to advance indeed.

What are you expected to give pertaining to your office? Remember that any system where people are there just for the sake of what they can get will sooner or later crash. No business can survive for long when employees are only there for what they can get. In other way round, no economy of any nation can endure for long when its citizens are all interested in plundering and pillaging its profit and resources. Output and values should exceed the input; this is the law of business that must hold even right in the public sector if sustainability is in the heart of the drivers and stakeholders. It is relevant to say here that an economy to which people put in more sacrifices and support to build will grow bigger.

When you take too much you kill initiatives. This is the secret of greatness: giving. You will be long remembered by what you give not what you take.

Your life is the input while your impact is your output. Your life only grows and becomes relevant to the extent of impact you are committed to make. Having enough to eat, drink and merry about is the beginning; but affecting others is the ultimate. Most people exist merely to eat, drink, merry and die.

What is your life worth? The measure of worth is impact. Life is a network; that is, a common system where we work together and wherein our works are connected.

We are connected to each other through a web-like structure. Whatever we do, affects somebody, and that somebody affects another who in turn affects another; the ripple effect continues and the human mere transitory senses can hardly fathom the reach. A single act can ripple to affect hundreds, thousands and millions directly or indirectly.

In the instance where the funds meant for weapons for soldiers to fight insurgence and terrorism are being misappropriated by a handful, it means the weapons are not bought, terrorists are better armed than soldiers, then civilians and soldiers are killed. Their families that depended on them become destitute.

When these terrorists overrun towns and villages, lives and properties are lost, commercial activities are crumbled, national GDP reduces, then more money not budgeted has to be pumped again to get another set of weapons for the soldiers, while other sectors like health, education and even workers' salaries are affected. This further generate more boomerangs as peoples go hungry, unemployment increases, crime rate increases among young men, girls go into prostitution and so on.

The ramifications of the devastating effects of the misappropriation and laundering of public funds are just wide and ever expanding.

The Conspiracy

Due to economic recession as a result of fall in crude oil price in the international market, exhaustion of foreign reserves, huge debt servicing and long years of unchecked corruption, Nigeria citizens have been exposed to one of the most traumatic experiences they have ever had in the recent years.

Year-in-year-out people steal, embezzle and corruptly misappropriate public fund for personal end. Over the years, it seemed that there would always be available resources to steal but suddenly there was an international conspiracy on the price of oil as it slumped to about a quarter of its most recent high price. The sudden and overwhelming slump could not be explained by economy of supply and demand. Nigeria was not the only nation affected by this price slump but Nigeria felt it the most because of years of mismanagement of oil money and looting of public funds.

We suddenly found out that we have no reserved fund, and that we failed to diversify the economy from oil in the time of surplus. This made me remember Professor Niyi Osundare's poem on this theme: "Eating Tomorrow's Yam". When the future comes there is no food left in the ban.

Though, only few people are guilty of massive looting, but the pain was felt in every corner. Salaries were unpaid, amenities going into state of disrepair, hunger and poverty everywhere and thousands began to die as a result of hunger, trauma, health challenges, and many other negative outflows because there is scarcity of fund to maintain the minimum lifestyle required for their survival. One way or the other, the distant relatives and dependants of those looters were also affected. This is an evil boomerang: few people stashed away the riches of the nation at the detriment of millions, the negative impact felt everywhere.

Let us imagine that things were done differently. Let us think that we have leaders who have the mind for their followers and working for the betterment of the citizens and advancement of the nation, they would have ploughed back the excess crude oil surplus to create alternative economy. Such diversification could be into agricultural development, tourism development, manufacturing, infrastructural development and enabling environment for small scale enterprises to grow. If done well, it would have attracted more foreign investments because investors' primary drive is right environment to create thriving ventures. Ultimately, millions of jobs would have been created and less dependence would have been placed on oil or the government, and we would definitely have had the grit to withstand the recent price slumps of crude oil like every other advanced economy of nations did.

A reference to this is the economy of United Arab Emirate (U.A.E.) wherein the popular Dubai City is situated. Dubai has become the fair haven of tourism of which few decades ago was merely an undeveloped city in the desert; but with good insight, funds derived from the nation's crude oil sales; one of the most beautiful cities in the world was built. So far, it has become the world center for tourism.

U.A.E. did not stop there; they have begun to further diversify their economy by growing their production and manufacturing sectors, human capacity development and enabling environment for businesses and investors: they refused to be caught in the web of religious extremism which many nations in that region are in.

Because they got it right, it has translated into a richer life for millions of citizens and the international community: a boomerang. When a person gets it right, does rightly and makes his world of contact better, it has a way of making life better for his immediate family, society, nation and sometime the international community. In the same light, evil spread from a source. Do you know that international scale terrorism started with certain individuals from some remote parts of the world? These individuals come together and grow into messengers of death.

Start something worthwhile and see it grow with time. Failing to stand for what is right is to allow evil to breed.

Find a vision for life and grow it into a network. You may know where and how it starts but you can't tell how far it will grow. See to it that you have a noble vision for life and ensure that this vision grows beyond you: this is the boomerang.

Always remember that your vision is beyond you; find those it is meant to serve and build a network on the premise.

If every one of us would make up his mind to direct his strength, talent, authority, capability and resources towards serving others, there would not be need to go to war, conflict will cease, poverty will almost be non-existent and sicknesses will be reduced.

When we strive to take more than our dues, we are calling for war and conflict. But when we give, we invite the world to become our friend indeed.

Poverty is an offshoot of trying to live a small life (not giving); when you think of others you will want to put extra efforts to make more in order to give more. Poverty is also as a result of certain people taking over more than is due to them and thereby creating scarcity for others; although this is a secondary kind of poverty. The primary kind of poverty is when individuals fail to take responsibility for their lives and sustenance. A good place for government of nations to start from is the empowerment of its citizens to do more not less.

Let us do more and give more. The world will soon realize that a new giant has been given birth to when a society begin to give more than it takes. This will bring a rebirth to governance, policies, serving, work ethics and sector reforms.

Government cannot do everything on its own, the government and the world needs your contributions.

A healthy society is one in which the individuals take up responsibility to make the best use of their lives towards service to God and humanity. Giving and service should be the core by which every religious creed is projected.

Wake up, you are like the sun; you have to shine on your fellow men. You are the answer unto many, and the change Nigeria needs.

Chapter Four

WHY GOVERNMENT FAILS

It is stupidity to keep doing things the same old way and expect a change. To get a different kind of result would require new kind of thinking, strategies and actions.

I believe it is easy to see through the cause of failed government or failed policy. One primary cause of such failure is ownership status; herein certain individuals take up exclusive power or authority to decide the fate of the rest. To them, leadership is one way path design which everyone else must adjust and comply to!

Such persons failed to realize that there can never be a government without a people and there can never be a community of people without a government. Government is a collective bargain and should never be forced on the people. In addition, a true government should be a creation of the people or their representatives. In the same light, policies that would sail through should have the people's endorsement either directly or through their representatives. On this platform, enduring and sustainable programs would score high in acceptability before all the major stakeholders which include the government, the citizens and their representatives. Also important driver of sustainable project is the private sector.

Conceding Power to the People

Any government any day and anytime will continue to hit its waterloo as long as it believes it can orchestrate and force down on the people its vision, policies and programs. The people for whom change is designed must always be in the mainstream of development. A successful public vision would always soar on the wings of collective participation. It is not what the government did that endures but what the people participated in. In a civilized setting, when the leaders conceive an idea they find a way to sell it to the people, they even allow for counter idea, at the end of the day, a referendum is called, the citizen come out to vote for or against the idea and at the end of the entire exercise, the voice of the people is allowed to stay. The most recent example of this is the Brexit. Upon losing the referendum to the opposition party, David Cameron, the British PM honorably stepped down for Theresa May whose side won.

Nothing can be sustained until it becomes a culture of the people. One cannot successfully root out corruption until a new culture of honesty, sincerity and transparency is entrenched as a lifestyle of the people. Therefore, we cannot adopt a fire brigade top-down decision and expect it to become a rallying point for the people.

Great leaders have the secret of conceding power to those under them and in so doing become extraordinary leaders. This is the secret of Alexander the Great; though a young man, he used this strategy to raise equally strong generals: Cassander, Ptolemy, Antigonus and Seleucus, the four of them kept his legacy such that after his death the vast Grecian empire was divided into four upon which they each ruled.

David, the most notable king in the history of Israel used this concept. He raised equally strong leaders from ordinary folks who in turn raised an army of strong soldiers and a nation that was revered all around. Israel was never known in history to have rise in national prominence before and after David the king. It was his time Israel became greatly enlarged.

You cannot raise weak leaders and citizens and expect a towering nation. Any wise thinking leader should know that the change he wants is pivotal on citizens' participation. To know this is to have a good start. To miss at this point is to be set for a colossal failure right from the start. Remember that the nation is composed of the citizens.

Four pictures I created to illustrate the state of nations.

Giant Leaders, Giant Citizens

The first is nations of giants: These are composed of strong leaders and strong citizens. Everybody is empowered to work dependently or independently for the advancement of the nation, seeking their common and individual interests without bowing down to restrictions. The citizens do not have to wait for a government watchdog before they do what is right. They take the responsibility to do what is right and to protect their common heritage. In such a society, citizens work toward a successful governance and the government is preoccupied with creating better living for its people. The people should create the kind of government they want with a purpose to have it serve them; any other idea of government is the corrupted version.

The best description of a nation in this category in recent history is America. If you take a study of America's greatness as a state you will find out that her greatness is not composed of extraordinary deed of certain super-heroes, politicians or statesmen. Take any sector such as governance, technology, medicine, manufacturing, or any other sector at world level, you will find an American leading the pack. They are the big game players at the global stage. America is great because individual American strives for greatness. The citizens are culturally empowered, thus they naturally manifest extraordinary feats at global level.

The society where giants lead giant is the peak of civilization. In the perfect form we can call such the utopian state. But in reality, we can apply it relatively. This means that certain society may get it right economically and yet be morally bankrupt. Nations should strive to be empowered and powerfully driven on every front both at government and individual level.

Giants Leaders, Dwarf Citizens

The second kind of society is one in which giants lead dwarfs. In the history of certain nations, they are fortunate to have emergence of extraordinary leaders dedicated to moving the nation forward and in the process plant a new culture that would empower the nation and overtime translate the non-empowered dwarfs into new breeds of giant.

The risk with this kind of society is that changes achieved cannot be sustained for long and the work of the leader is like writing on the water if there is no enough time to entrench the new change as a culture.

The America of today was once in this class. America was once a colony under the British Empire, a dwarf nation with dwarf citizenry. But within it was a class of thoughtful leaders like George Washington, Thomas Jefferson and host of others who motivated her independence and planted within them the seed of greatness as can be seen in the United States Declaration of Independence by Thomas Jefferson, Benjamin Franklin, Roger Sherman, John Adams and Robert Livingston. These people forged a new meaning, mind set and status for the people of America.

The antithesis of giants leading dwarfs in my own opinion can be seen with regards to the exploit of Thomas Sankara of Burkina Faso and Muammar Gaddafi of Libya.

Thomas Sankara was viewed as a charismatic icon with ambitious programs to eliminate corruption and the dominance of the former French colonial influence. His primary goals were social and economic change which he even started by renaming the country from Upper Volta to Burkina Faso meaning Land of Upright men, the name the country still maintain till date but before he could entrench the new goals, ideologies and values for a transformed nation, he was assassinated by Blaise Campaore along with 13 members of his cabinet who could have in future try to actualize the vision in his absence. It was a total cleansing off the sand of his vision and prospects for his country. The action sank the nation back to its old state.

It would have been a different story if Thomas Sankara had been able to create a new culture among his leadership team and citizens. Blaise Campaore being able to succeed such a heroic leader, though a villain himself is alarming; taking over after the assassination and he ruled long enough from 1987-2014. This shows that the people were not empowered to sustain the dream of Thomas Sankara. If they were empowered as citizens, the likes of Blaise Campaore would not find it comfortable to be in power for so long. Any government exists because the people endure it long enough.

Muammar Gaddafi may be seen in a bad light by the Western nations but he succeeded in many ways that matter to the poor and marginalized people of Libya. While many quarters may see him as a dictator, he stood out as one of the most benevolent leaders in African regions: he is a man who looked out for the citizens. Libya economy was exceptionally impressive. He ruled for a long stretch of period from 1969 – 2011.

He was a dominant leader who failed to raise equally strong personalities within his domain. He ruled that ancient nation of Libya for a little more than 40 years yet failed to raise powerful leaders in his stead. After he was killed in 2011, this nation sank and retrogressed. This means that Gaddafi was a giant who was comfortable to lead his pack of dwarfish followers.

Another dangerous part to this image of a strong leader is that when the enemy wants to get within such a territory, all they need do is remove the strong leader. Insinuation had it that Gaddafi's downfall was masterminded by the West.

In extreme cases, a strong leader can be destroyed by his own people whom he is working to sustain. The simple reason is that the average mind rarely knows what or who is in his best interest. Strong leaders often have the big and complete picture which sometime may require leading the dwarf minds through momentary inconveniences over a stretch of time. Average citizens in underdeveloped world often fight every possible inconvenience; without patience the people often jeopardize the great vision of the leader.

Here is an example in Nigeria; many of us recognize the presence of some cabals who cash in on oil subsidy to make themselves rich at the expense of the citizens. Though the citizens knew they were being short-changed by this cabals yet they insist that oil subsidy should remain. They jeopardized the long term win in the conversion of the gain of oil subsidy removal into infrastructure work. The people would rather side with the cabals and create campaigns of calumny against their leaders. Some leaders may be corrupt which create distrust in the hearts of the people, but all leaders through successive governments will not be corrupt at all times to want to insist on the removal of oil subsidy. Time will reveal the truth much plainly.

The truth about life is that the masses rarely have access to the big picture.

The Dwarf Leaders and Giant Citizens

I will not talk much on this because it is not a common scenario to have a dwarf leader and giants as followers. This is an aberration. It is an accidental kind of system whereby circumstances thrust a weak person into leadership status. Such do happen at the instance of the death of a strong leader who has around him a weak lieutenant who seizes on the occasion. Another reason why a weak person can find himself rule over stronger people is structural royal system of successor and structured organization or society that follows a prescribed successor process without regard to strength.

In such a society, the weak leader will not last except some very strong leaders hold forte for him and are benefitting from his weakness. He may also stay long if he builds up strength and establish himself over time. If the unusual happened and he sustained himself long enough as a weakling, this will weary the strength of the people and dilute their capability; sooner or later the society will become like the leader.

Every society has had a taste of such at one time or the other, but it is important to note that progressive societies have ways of turning away weak leaders through legislation, election, and sack and selection process.

This is one of the errors propagated by the quota system of selection which is as old as Nigeria. The British while leaving planted this ominous poison to dilute the strength of Nigeria. Many may argue or refuse to acknowledge the insanity of quota or zoning system of selection especially in leadership. When you place the weak ahead of the strong, the two will weary each other; nobody can give what he does not have.

The Nation of Dwarfs

The fourth kind of society is one in which a dwarf rules over a community of dwarfs. This is the worst state any society can be because there is no way their condition can improve.

The irony of it is that they represent the most satisfied class of people in spite of lack, poverty and deprivations. I do not mean comfortable, I mean satisfied with the status quo. No one is stretching or challenging them to become better or do more; no sacrifice and no discipline among the leadership and the citizenry.

This is the state of most third world nations. Everybody is satisfied and no one wants the boat of status quo to be rocked. They are culturally bent towards vicious lifestyles of corruption, dishonesty and self-serving propensity. The problem is that their ravaging tendency may lead to the extinct or subjugation of such society. History has it on one side that dinosaurs went into extinction because of their ravenous propensity which caused imbalance in the ecology. The fragile ecology of the time could not sustain dinosaurs' ravenous appetite and they went into extinction for this reason. No matter the size, any nation that fails to adapt upward will soon crumble.

The nation of Nigeria sadly sits comfortably in this category with people celebrating mediocrity and lack of principle in leadership. This is why we are much satisfied to raise insincere leaders who know how to deceive us, to give us what we want and not what we need.

True leadership is dedicated to serve the people's needs and not their wants. There is a world of difference between needs and wants.

We are a people who want something for nothing. We want infrastructure development yet will vote for a leader who will subsidize everything. We cannot eat tomorrow's yam today and still look for a harvest when the tomorrow arrives. We want subsidy, many of the so called politicians know this and they use it as bait to bargain their mandates, steal our votes and also to loot the nation's treasury!

While other nations are working hard to build a strong economy; exporting to us the product of their own citizens for our consumption, we are here crying like spoilt children that our borders should remain opened for influx of those foreign goods. Any government that closes the border in order to make us look inward and improvise is seen as no friend to the citizens. So the people allow for weak leaders who will pamper their mediocrity.

Recently, a leader arose who began to block the loopholes that prospered weak economy. Major areas looked into include importation, subsidy and tax. Unfortunately, when you close borders to importation without commensurate local production, price hike of such goods is inevitable. Presumably, the government by closing the border to certain goods intended to motivate the people to produce their own goods but the people fought hard against this. They also fought against removal of oil subsidy. And they keep fighting against every inconvenience instead of using the harsh situations to forge new meaning for living; like spoilt children they keep whining when they could not lay hands on free things.

Yoruba has this adage: iya o je e o ni o gbon. This means you have not suffered, yet you claim to be wise. No nation attained greatness without sacrifice, struggles and inconveniences as bedrock.

The longing for free things is the bait to slavery. Great people take responsibility to create the world they want.

When the citizens lose access to free things they began to cry: In desperation the people began to lament for the return of the corruption laden era of past leaders. The people failed to recognize that nothing good comes with ease, there is a price for greatness; the price of sacrifice, discipline, honesty and hard work are pivotal to development of individuals and the societies.

Any society that fails to have its government invest in the empowerment of its citizens is only getting itself set for trouble in the nearest future.

Change and transformation can never be achieved on the wing of the leadership alone; it takes both wings of the leadership and citizenry to fly. There must be mutual understanding, purpose and vision. Therefore, the leadership class should shift from propaganda to intense education and development of the citizens; and with the understanding that the greatest empowerment to be set rolling is that which is aimed at transforming the mind.

A transformed and highly developed mind is the greatest gift that can be bequeathed to a generation. A people may be situated in the desert, but with the right use of their mind they would soon transform it to a prosperous haven. And in transforming the people's mind is the need to let them understand the difference between virtues and vices, the consequences of their choices, and the economic importance of every action on the nation now and in the far future.

Leaders need to understand that their empowered state of mind has to be imparted to the followers; and conversely, empowered citizens should always ensure that their choice of leaders will lead to advancement.

Taking A Look At Autocratic Government:

An autocratic government may seem impressive with performance but the success recorded is often short lived. A dictator will often coax and force every of his doctrine down the throat of the people. Autocrats make people do things in certain ways without giving them the why.

When people don't know why they do what they do, whatever they do will only be for a short while, more so without sustainability. They do the right thing as long as the leader is around. The basics of a model of change should be understood with clarity by the laymen in any society, devoid of any complexity. A clarion call towards a vision or cause should be clear to all the stakeholders and subjects.

Again, let us look at Thomas Sankara and Muamar Gaddafi. The two of them controlled state elements much through the use of force (both with military background) than persuasion. What they chose to achieve were achieved and sustained - as long as they were in power.

On the other hand, American leaders historically empowered its citizens from generation to generation through mutual understanding and cooperation. This was why most of the values of the founding fathers were kept unto this day. Autocratic change is one way, from top downward without consensus feedback from the people; and without consensus or collective agreement the citizens will see the idea, vision or policy as government's idea and not everybody's.

Meaningful change cannot be achieved until the people learn to take responsibilities and see that their input is vital to the survival of the system and more, it is appreciated. The people must see themselves as important factor in creating the change the nation needs and they must be empowered; empowerment which consists of provision of an environment conducive for the growth of noble aspirations of citizens to become the best they can ever become and such noble aspirations which must align with their personalities, talents, and peculiarities: not to shortchanged them but to enhance their innate drive.

A government that empowers its people to achieve more will always thrive any day.

Chapter Five

VITAL PREJUDICES TO DEAL WITH

This chapter is a follow up on the preceding one on why government fails. The same reason why government fails can be adduced to why many branding and re-branding program are not getting through. Branding are empowerment messages or activities that help to change the perception of people to think or act in certain positive way.

Once one has succeeded in changing someone's perceptions, it becomes easy to make him act in line with the new set of knowledge, understanding and belief. Someone's perception has a way of affecting the use of new knowledge and idea.

National branding is a design to make a shift from old non-effective cultures into a more progressive way of life and thinking through repeated sets of actions. We need to reaffirm culture in its broad definition as a way of life of a people.

Most times, we look at culture from the perspective of our traditions and our local lifestyles to our dances; this is the idea and definition of culture. Yet, in its broader sense, culture is a dominant and common lifestyle that pervades in any given society.

Laziness, fun-seeking, merry making could describe a people; so it becomes a culture. Corruption, bribery, and public stealing could be a culture elsewhere. Whatever way of life that is generally acceptable or practicable in a society becomes a form of culture.

Retrogressive and underdeveloped society certainly adopted some vices as culture which makes it difficult to advance. A society may be deeply involved in graft and corruption that you can see it from one border end to another as it is not unfamiliar to Nigeria. This is noted as a revealing trend, we don't need to deceive ourselves by pretending that it is not there.

I heard appalling stories of certain ministers and top leaders in government circle who were saddled with the change responsibility but go about in the same old dirty lifestyle of budget padding, high handedness, contract frauds and many more. There is a case of a well respected minister who upon assuming office brought in several registered firms in the name of some of his accomplices. He defrauded the nation by awarding many of the contracts to his accomplices.

We do not need to shy away from it; corruption is Nigeria's big problem. We need to face it, call it by its name and deal with it as a vice that it is. You can never solve an issue if you pretend that it is not there.

Every nation that wants upward transformation would need to isolate its predominant vice that has presented itself as a culture. Such vice has to be understood in view of its detrimental effects and loses it incurs on the society with proofs and data. On the other side the new values required to replace the old vices should be studied: its benefits, case studies and models to be brought to limelight. This should be done with clarity and simplicity for all to learn and emulate from.

The new vision, ideal or virtue should turn to a rallying point and such virtue should be well rewarded and the vices punished. When vices are overlooked, re-branding campaigns become mere government propaganda. An ancient king, Solomon said: when evil is overlooked, vices multiply and a society tends toward anarchy.

For instance, exam malpractice is frowned at in concept but we do know that it is on the increase by the day in the academic sector. It is on the increase because offenders are rarely punished. A shift in lifestyle requires orientation, but reorientation must be coupled with reward for those who adopt it and a punishment for those who want to maintain the old retrogressive lifestyle.

An old cultural value is not easy to overhaul, there must be a driver for the new value. The driver is the dialectic twin of reward and punishment. If you identify the vices stunting national or societal growth, as a leader you cannot overlook offenders, by doing the contrary, you are not being fair to the larger society because if the offender has his way without a reprisal he would corrupt the rest members of the society – in no time.

Sometime ago, we had an unprecedented case of embezzlement of such outrageous proportions in which pension funds amounting to staggering billions of Naira was siphoned. I bet many Nigerians would have forgotten by now – probably because another unprecedented outrageous level of embezzlement in the highest places has occurred and kind of shadowed that. The culprit I suspect bribed his way through to the judges: he was given the option to pay a meager sum which was a far cry from the amount he was said to have embezzled, to pay less than a million Naira fine as against going to jail for the embezzled billions of Naira. This is an example of using kids' glove to deal with societal vices. With such acts of impunity, no amount of noise in the name of re-branding can change any one perception for the good; instead it will embolden other offenders.

Can we really imagine the havoc of pension scam on the lives of tens of thousands? I have pensioners around me; many of them are incapacitated, weak, old and frail to engage in any kind of job. To embezzle their fund is to literally send thousands of them to early grave. If government leaders can rightly imagine the gravity of those vices we uphold in this nation, I think we should have a rethink on effectively overhauling the old regressive cultures of corruption.

The second example is what is termed plea bargains. This is the soft landing privilege of the rich, the powerful and politicians alike. When they steal or embezzle funds and are caught, they are to come to the table, plead for leniency, and then give back any reasonable amount they could afford. We have cases of states governors who were indicted with corrupt charges of not less than fifty billion; many of them barely coughed out as much as five billion Naira. This was done in the name of plea bargains. Afterward, they were freed in every sense it.

By allowing corrupt people to walk around freely without commensurate punishment is to aid the growth of the vice. Shift in cultural values requires administration of punitive measures and eternal vigilance to ensure everyone is doing the right thing.

Dealing With Sentiments

To effectively create a re-brand of the nation, the pivotal area to look at is the sentiments of the citizens. We know many of our sentiments to be vices but we never agreed that those same sentiments are the factors responsible for retrogression of the nation.

The Biggest Sentiment: Corruption

Average Nigerian doesn't believe that corruption is a major problem why we have kept our place in the bottom of the table of highly performing economies in the world. Corrupt leaders have literally crumbled the Nigerian nation. A president made an attempt to probe past leaders with regard to misappropriation of funds but surprisingly, many well meaning citizens and ordinary folks kicked against it. My own position is this: if you do not punish the erring ones, how do you correct those who are hell bent on keeping the status quo?

Corruption is Nigeria biggest sentiment that a president was infamously quoted as saying that "corruption is not stealing". It may have been an off-guard statement, then following on the heel of this on the social media are citizens vetoing corruption to go on if only prices of food, exchange rate and so on will come down. Many Nigerians have not yet understood the simple fact that corruption is the major cause of underdevelopment, poverty and inflation. Research by The World Bank Group and IMF indicates strong correlations between corruption and underdevelopment.

"In the developing world, corruption is public enemy number one," said Jim Yong, a World Bank Group President.

Kim described the effects of corruption on developing countries. "Every dollar that a corrupt official or a corrupt business person puts in their pocket is a dollar stolen from a pregnant woman who needs health care; or from a girl or a boy who deserves an education; or from communities that need water, road, and schools."

He further by citing three key elements in the World Bank Group's approach:

"First, we need to improve the way we share and apply knowledge about building institutions with greater integrity; second, we need to empower citizens with information and tools to make their governments more effective and accountable; and third, we need to build a global movement to prevail over corruption."

Source: (www.worldbank.org/en/news/press-release/2013/12/19/corruption-developing-countries-world-bank-group-president-kim)

Corruption is an obnoxious cancer that is fast and furiously spreading to other healthy parts of our great Nigerian nation and it must be exposed and expunged from our system.

Religious Sentiments

The next sentiment is religion. Generally, I see many religious views as perception built up from information gathered which are not necessarily by the scriptures or written guides of the religion.

Certain religious positions are taken as a result of parental background, sectarian views are also fallout from religious leaders in a certain society. Many of our beliefs are handed over to us without being questioned by us.

This should be enough to humble us: that we are not the creator of most religious views we hold on to. Many have Islamic background so the child turns out a Moslem and many have Christianity background so the child turns out a Christian. Then why should we boast of things we do not create?

My personal view is that religion or spiritual affiliation should be a means to understand the mind of the Creator for a useful or beneficial outcome to the universe and our immediate environment. Religious belief should make us better human beings, sacrificing, giving and respecting our neighbour's fundamentals rights; not turning into a terrorists sect or a sort of extremist.

Any religious beliefs that bring down others and cause the destruction of our world should be dropped; in other way round, we should embrace the code of our religion that creates prosperity, procreation, abundance and security of lives. We should also bear in mind that the gifts of nature and opportunities are offered equally to all mankind. God makes his rain to fall on the good and the evil. God's benevolence is unto all men. So why should anyone limit another person because he did not belong to the same religious affiliation?

The good God is a benevolent one. The worthy religious position should dispense good work to all.

Check it out: every nation on earth has its own repository gift, resources, values and riches irrespective of religious view. The final outcome for harnessing the good gifts of God rests on our choices of actions; which are on either side of the divide of vices or virtues, not our religious inclinations. Individuals and nations determine their fate by their faith: a faith which is beyond religion – a faith in vices or virtues.

In spite of abundance – of mineral and human resources - Nigeria wallows in underdevelopment, not because we are not religious but because we celebrate vices above principles entrenched in godliness and righteousness.

Many people become profane and kinsmen of the devil by reason of their religious sentiments. It is an ugly religious vice for each religion to struggle for dominance over the other. Nigeria is indeed a failed test laboratory of religion's tolerance when we take a view at the religious bigotry and sentiments instead of ideological path of reasoning.

The citizens fall out on each other and vote based on such (religion) sentiments. Merit is sacrificed on the altar of religion; and stealing mandates for religion's sake. Every religion wants to have the largest pile of the presidency, legislators and various leadership positions and offices even when they have to plant a mere stooge or nincompoop as a representative of their religious idiosyncrasies. A religious practice that worth its salt will be fair to distribute resources and leadership to all citizens based on merit. Religion should not be synonymous with mediocrity, slavery and opportunism.

A society can never advance beyond its level of honour for merit. Effective re-branding starts with breaking the wall of religious sentiments in Nigeria, and as a major vice that must be dealt with.

Tribal and Ethnic Sentiments

The third kinds of sentiments which often lock horn in preeminence with religious sentiments are tribal and ethnic sentiments. I have interacted with many individuals from various groups, and a major prejudice is the air of superiority each exuded. The Barbarian from a given tribe sees himself better than the most cultured personality from another tribe. Come Election Day, they would rather vote for their own goat, than a technocrat from another tribe; even when they know that their own goat will eat their yams: this is the depth of folly and chasm created in view of tribal sentiments.

Racial, tribal or ethnic sense of supremacy has caused much evil than good and has led to countless destruction of lives and properties; it is also a factor in slavery, colonialism and neo-colonialism. So it is, tribal and ethnic sentiments are vital factors to retrogressions.

Racial prejudice caused the Second World War where Hitler led the murder of more than six million Jews and millions from other nations around the world also died as a result. In this same like, Rwanda genocide was an evil spectacle that prospered under ethnic divides. Several other form of ethnic cleansing are secretly taking place in some parts of Northern Nigeria but nobody dared called it so.

Through tribal and ethnic sentiments we have polluted the rank of our national leadership, affected the morals of our officers and put in round pegs in square holes; we hope to get better. Strength should match strength and ability should match ability: each (tribe or ethnic groups) should give up trying to match weakness with strength and instead build on its own endowment, strength and ability.

Here is an evasive challenge our lazy minded leaders have not been able to proffer answer to: ability to provide a better alternative to quota system, we have clear distributive quota system but nothing about contributive quota system. If we are clear about sharing wealth to reflect on land mass, people and population, we should have similar measure to ensure even contribution from every zone and citizens. A true federation is one with a balance in input and output from all its constituency and regions.

New leaders in national politics should begin to create better alternatives of federation if we want the nation to really move forward.

Here is an experience of my dad about quota system:

Years ago, I was in primary school. My dad came back from the office dissatisfied and bordered about something. He narrated how a superintendent of police from one of the tribes could not read or write in the official language of the federal job. My dad who was a far junior, an inspector was detailed to read and write for his boss. I saw the look of frustration on the face of my dad; even my young mind knew it was bad, and this was in the early 80s, therefore, quota system did not start today.

This made me remembered two incidents again while in the primary school. I had a teacher who I will like to call Mr. "M" who did not just feel like honouring me with the first position as a result of an ulterior motive well known to him. He has a favourite big girl in my class. In those days, you will sometime find girls who are well beyond puberty in primary school. He couldn't build scores for his favourite through the regular subjects like Mathematics and English-language so he went on to cut my score by half in a craft subject we called "Hand Work" in those days and gave full mark to the big girl in the class. I came second, and I cried home. The headmaster looked into the issue and has to reprimand the teacher for the injustice. He never repeated such.

If only Nigeria will find her own upstanding and dutiful "headmasters"; the tears of the shortchanged little masters (experts and superior minds) that have been pushed to the background by the Mr. "Ms" in our public offices and the society at large would long have been wiped away.

No matter the explanation or justification, it does not appeal to the school of common sense to promote the weak above the strong. A real federal system should translate to matching ability: a superintendent from one region should match a superintendent from another. Nepotism, ethnocentrism and tribal sentiments have weakened the Federal Character; to promote weaklings as a way of contributing to a federation is an evil in itself.

Without a true balance of give and take, a society is sure on the path of rottenness.

We cannot keep deceiving ourselves with inequality in competence. This factor is hugely responsible for mediocrity that has grown out of proportion in our civil service system. If the boss does not know better than his subordinate, complacency is inevitable because the driver himself is directionless. In addition, when reward is inequitably shared, the wronged person tends to withdraw from giving his best.

Our quota system is a bandwagon, it will get us nowhere. The truth has to be said sometime and even now, though it may not be appealing.

Quota system is orchestrated by the West nations and the injury afflicted by the leadership on all. The psychology of the incompetent leader is challenged all his life when he has to depend on his subordinate before he can act. Inwardly, the incompetent leader suffers the agony of incompetence and the embarrassment of having to wait on the subordinate for answer instead of the other way round. Also, his subordinate do suffers from non-motivating work environment that withdraw his due reward because he is from the wrong side of the tribal divide.

Beneath, there is an unseen balance of equity that connects man to man and makes everyone a custodian of ability and competence; we are all equal in some ways, though ability may differ. The work of the leader is not to trade citizen's competence in the name of satisfying a federal character but instead to help each citizen to become the best in their line of competence. It is a loss to a nation to draft a contented farmer to the police force just because you want to complete a quota system.

Why not empower the farmer to be the best farmer he can ever be? Give him an enabling environment, boost his morale and empower him through possible means to maximize his vocation; then he will be happy with himself and his nation. By so doing he will do much more better because he is in his native field of competence. A tribe may not have a large number of policemen like another tribe, but would be glad in that they are rich in other ways as contributor to national wealth.

An American farmer will never trade his place to seek for a white collar job somewhere. The mind set should be empowered to seek to advance in one's competence and to become the best therein.

Taking critical look; every jostling and struggle is about taking and taking from the center. In trying to take from the center we have ruined what was left. We were once rich, then every tribe was showcasing its trades and capability but we grow to become poor and lean. We left our primary place and we all jostled after vanity so much that a man will so abandon his native heritage, homeland, family and religious affiliations to adopt the one he feels is thriving and more favoured in the country.

A nation become rich when each segment, group, ethnicity and tribe contribute what it has to the center; and becomes poor when everyone wants to take.

An advancing society is one in which everyone is giving (offering) the best he has; with adequate knowledge that his contribution to the federation is not inferior. Any tribe that is contributing inferior resources to the center is cheating on others; they are unfair and bad section of the nation.

Finally, on issue of quota system, we may try to excuse it that it has served its usefulness in time past, but now it is evident that it is an inferior tool to take us to the new height of national prosperity and international prominence; so far we have not seen the success in a quota system as being practiced here in Nigeria.

If no private organization will parade unskilled hands in the name of regionalism, it is irresponsibility of our nation to fill her leadership position with people who are mediocre and expect a transformed society. We need to begin to overhaul quota system in any rebranding exercise we want to undertake. Let each tribe or ethnic group go back to the drawing board to see how best they can serve the common interest in a non-competitive spirit.

We can showcase strength and contribution in more creative ways than using a quota system. A good federation is an exchange platform not a competition platform.

Resource Control

Resource control is another issue of grave concern. Plundering one region to salvage the poverty of another should not be the thinking of a federal system. You cannot heal the poverty of a region by taking from another, instead you are brewing more indolence and the final state of poverty of the weaker region will be worse. A poor man can only be transformed by a new thinking of possibility and industry; a belief in self that he has what is required to make a new desirable world for himself.

I so much believe in resource control of regions and contribution to the central government from time to time. I am saying this from the insight that no state, tribe or region is actually poor. The poverty we have in many parts is a reflection of failure to look inward, homeward and to the abundant resources in each ones domain.

Our situation is compounded by our leaders and citizens propensity for quick money which crude oil readily offers. To this I will say: our possession of crude oil will turn to a curse if we refuse to harness other potential resources. There should be a balanced contribution of resources to the center. Why should the leaders be too lazy to think and sweat out the desirable outcome of greatness and why would every citizen wait on crude oil revenue without personal contribution to the nation's growth?

If one region is responsible for the supply of 90 percent of a nation's income, this may breed dissatisfaction overtime which if not corrected, may lead to serious state of anarchy. But if a region is supplying 90 percent to the federation account for the purpose of using these resources to harness wealth from other regions in order to yield a multiplying effect on a growing economy, all the parties involved will be happy about this. But this is not the case in Nigeria, ours is a consumerist nation where everybody brings his own knife to cut from the "national cake".

This analogy will make it simple enough to grab. I may be magnanimous enough to help a poor young graduate for a while; feed him, clothe him and cater for his needs. But a time will come that I will expect him to be empowered enough to fend for himself. If he wants to continue living freely on my income, we may end up with fallout because eventually, my income will not be eternally available for his free use. In the same way, a country should not expect her vast resources to come from one section for years and expect peaceful coexistence.

For effective national re-branding, we should drift more towards resource control by sections and regions of the nation. In the new re-branding, there should be a conscious motivation for individual and regional discoveries where every side comes to the center table with a valuable contribution in terms of resources. In a business relationship, every partner has something to offer

When you share goods equally between the strong and the weak you end up creating further weakness in the latter.

A professor proved this in one of his classes. In his first test everyone earned their respective mark based on merit. Before the next test he told them that henceforth, he would average their scores, meaning everyone would score the same average mark. The outcome was that the result favoured the poor students and they were happy about this while the brilliant students were not happy. In the third test the class average was a failure because everybody relaxed; no reward and motivation for hard work.

The professor thereby concluded that any economy that does not reward merit will go downward over time until the reward system is adjusted to capture a merit ground.

What resource control means is that a person who produces more should have more control on what he produces but by the time you give back a fraction to a region that produces a resources in the name of Federal Character or whatever you call it, you are breeding a monster of acrimony which will be unleashed someday.

Resource control is not a means to empower one region over the other; it is about following a natural order of things wherein one becomes fair in dealings and giving what is due to Caesar to Caesar. It is about equitable responsibility to the joint project called Nigeria. This is about each divide discovering self and becoming a contributor instead of being parasitic to the detriment of the health of the nation.

Resource control is about fostering competitive advantages among regions and creating an enterprising society whereby every region will use what it has to create wealth.

Japan cannot measure up with the abounding natural resources we have here in Nigeria yet they were able to create a surplus economy from her lean natural resources. Israel likewise was planted on a barren land when compared to our dear country yet was blessed and wealthy beyond measure. What are they doing that we failed to do?

In the final estimate, the level of human capital development will determine the extent of economic transformation of a nation. Leaders who embezzle are not well developed in their mind. Militants who blow power stations and oil pipelines are enemies to growth, no matter the justification. There can't be any justification for such barbarism.

Religious extremist who level cities and soak the land with blood of innocent women and children are detrimental to economic growth. Together, these classes are poorly developed human minds.

The real re-branding will put into consideration the development of the minds to embrace only patterns that enhance economic growth.

The emphasis remains: with human capital development every region has something to offer. Human capital development is more than going to school; it is more about integrating individuals to become contributors to national growth.

With a perverted mind, a professor could be injurious through wrong use of his knowledge, a judge can interpret the law to suit his selfish cause and a religion's leader could rear a devil's sect. Elitism has less to do with the transformation of an economy like having the right mind. Nigerians are one of the most educated nations of the world, but we are cultured with the wrong mind set which makes our educational knowledge to be applied in the wrong direction that supports retrogression. There are two sides to education as we have two sides to a coin. Education can build and it can destroy: education brought about the internet, nuclear power, and genetic engineering, all these have been abused by certain educated fellows to bring down the world value system as regard use of the internet, blowing up of cities as in nuclear power plant and breeding biological weapons using genetic engineering.

Yet if we chose to use our minds constructively, we can turn a desert into a world class tourist attraction.

Instead of fighting over resource control especially at the central government, let us unleash the minds of Nigerians to use what they have to bring the nation to prosperity and prominence among other nations of the world. The journey of a prosperous nation starts with the individual. And when the individuals begin to excel and regions begin to appreciate in wealth and the government is not a burden to them rather give them control and help them to protect the reward of their labour and resources, they will be glad to put in all their energy. When people are aware they are the custodian of their own prosperity, they will readily work harder to create more.

How should the government earn? It should be more through taxes, levies and royalties.

It may look unwise at the initial stage to cede resource control back to regions, states and individuals but by so doing you will be stabilizing the society and creating more wealth for the individual citizens, states, regions and ultimately the nation.

Government's primary responsibility is administration and governance; creation of wealth is her secondary function. Government should have no concern with resource control or doing business rather it should be contented with earning revenues through fair dealings. Government should cease from robbing Peter to pay Paul, instead teach Paul how to earn his own income and contribute meaningfully to the common partnership.

Having taken a look at some major prejudices and sentiments that have halted the nation's advancement, we need to brace up, drop the cloak of hypocrisy and pretense. Now, we all know the real debacle to national preeminence – I mean the already discussed sentiments. If any government leader is really desirous of growth, change and transformation they would need to look on how to put a check to such sentiments as corruption, religious sentiments, tribal or ethnic prejudices, and resource control.

If Nigeria wants to rise to the top in global dealings, governance has to be exercised without sentiments instead with fairness and equity to all.

Chapter Six

CASTING DOWN POLITICAL DIVIDES

Recently, I was discussing with a friend, he said it will be better if more states are created in Nigeria. According to him, by so doing, each of the new states will be more homogenously represented thereby bringing about more peace and stability in our already thin pulled system which in effect will translate to further development and transformation of each divide. But I replied: What good has the fragmentations and states creations done so far to the nation?

The problem of sectionalism has stayed as long as Nigeria has been a country and it is obviously a problem orchestrated by our founding fathers. From independence, our founding fathers were often quick to point out the difference between one tribe and the other but slow to point our common values and other qualities - both individually and collectively - that unite us.

This is why the younger generation finds it difficult to believe that we are one. The Nigerian Civil War (The Biafran War) was a case study: it was a battle of difference. Over the years, we have succeeded in creating one thing: reasons why one tribe, ethnic group, section and language is different from the other. This will continue until we find what unites us and then promote it above what divides us.

Small minds see why men are different, the big minds tend to find common ground to unite and advance together. This therefore means that when you see a leader who preaches division, tribal sentiments and the likes; he is weak and hiding behind sentiments to pull crowds to himself. This alone is an indication that he lacked the credibility to be a leader.

The 21st Century man or politician should be a man that unites and makes the community of men one big family in this global village. For we are beginning to see that the bigger conglomerates whether of society are averagely doing better; take a look at America and China. It is time we get out and refuse to take heed to such leaders that play at the brink of sectionalism and zoning; they have not done us any good, and by principle they will never have any good to offer our corporate existence than to hinder our common progress and advancement as a nation. Those who want to plunder us using divisive tactics will only make us smaller and weaker if we listen to them.

I want you to know that since the fall of Berlin Wall, racial and sectional leaders are fast becoming leprous hands no one wants to hold especially in the light of the huge atrocities of Adolf Hitler in promoting Nazism. Let Nigeria watch out for such elements that are prone to divisiveness. Nigeria is yet to do justice to the existence of the deep rooted tribalism which has been trailing us since independence. Come to think of it: If Obama could come up to rule an American nation hugely populated by Caucasians so why must one group in an African country believe that only their own bloc are more entitled to rule because they are majority while the minority go to hell or sit and watch them do it even if they fail at it; even when there is the possibility of getting a more competent candidate from the numerically disadvantaged group. Every man based on competence should have fair opportunity to aspire to any height of attainment whether in politics or private practice. For instance, why would an

Igbo man beg to get to the top because he is not from another end of the nation? Meanwhile, he had dwelled there, established a home, a business and probably married one of their own. To perpetually subjugate one group is to open up a crack in the system to divine anger. Lesson could be learnt from how slave trade was abolished in America and the heck of pain attributed to it through the American Civil War. It was after the abolition of slave trade by Abraham Lincoln that America was able to end the civil war. You cannot keep others down and expect to enjoy the upward life.

The world is changing, so let Nigeria change along and position herself to embrace true leadership where only credible people find their way to the top irrespective of their background, religion, tribe or language. If we fail to heed this call, we should not be disappointed when small African nations become more prominent than the supposed giant of Africa. At the end of the day, quality should weigh over quantity. It is not the size of a nation but the robustness of her people both in mental capability and opportunity to lead her that is far more important.

A country will rise or fall to the level of her leadership's competence. Everything boils down to leadership; therefore the need to implore everyone to support right leadership and no longer be lured into mediocrity through sectional or tribal sentiments; separationism is old fashion in this global village.

Pitching for a "Brother".

Sometimes I wonder why people go to any length to want their brother to be the one in power even in the face of obvious injustice. This shows how small minded, selfish, and ill-conceited we are to one another. It is a pointer to a fact: we have evil mind towards others when we want to put others down at all cost and we should be feared to be trusted with power because sectional leaders will end up oppressing the disadvantaged group one way or the other.

When there is trust and love which we preach as a nation and as religious people, then there should be no reason why we would not allow others to share in the exercise of leadership when they are competently qualified. If truly we are indeed religious, we would be more accommodating of others as we share our commonwealth with fairness and equity.

The fact that some groups agitate or tend to hold tightly to the instrument of power is a red light that we have not gotten leadership principle right in this part of the world. To negate a principle is to suffer the consequence/effect. This malady has taken a step further. Case in point, an individual submits a proposal to execute a project. Most Nigerian leaders abuse Intellectual Properties by shortchanging the proprietor and handing over the proposal to a kinsman or a close friend to doctor it and get the job – without any compensation or acknowledgment. They are so nefariously sick in the mind that they care less about the quality of any project being executed under their auspices so far it is their kin and kith doing it. A true leader should belong to all; and when a leader is not for everybody he has failed from the start, no matter the number of yes men he has around him.

A leader will arouse contempt, agitations and militancy among the ranks - in worst case, anarchy when it has become visible that the leader is self serving and protects the interest of one group above others as every other group will also struggle to plant their own person as the leader. This is one of the many reasons Nigeria has not had rest for as long as anyone could remember. Everyone is jostling for the center chair in order to have a piece of the cake. This further shows us why it will be hard to get credible candidates to fill our leadership seats: credible people are not self-serving, so they will have no need to want to divide the lot to win over others while on the other hand the corrupt ones will play the game of group interests, division and separation to the full. Thus, for this reason, it is very hard to field good leaders until the people learn not to fall into politicians' divide-and-rule antics.

Another way to see this rottenness is this: someone from one part of Nigeria could have a woeful political records, but if he could shout loudest to support sectionalism which in our present day language is referred to as zoning or quota then the political illiterates could easily be swept off their feet in frenzy to give their votes in spite of overwhelming facts of incompetence. The big question here: What have they gotten by continuous voting for their kith? Your real brother is not your tribesman but the one that caters for your need.

For a healthy nation, common interests should override sectional interests, and on that basis look for leaders who will protect the common uniting interests in fairness; this principle should reflect on our choices of the next president, governor, senator, chairman and so on and so forth. If you and I will ever have a nation we can be proud of, then we must close our eyes to our differences and gun for competence, capability and capacity of leadership. A credible candidate from the remotest place of our society will do us much good than someone who is our kin or tribe but who has none of our interests.

Who is your brother?

Brotherliness is more than bloodline connection. In a far reaching definition, a brother is he that has your utmost concern at heart and that want everything to be in your best interest favourably. Your brother is he that seeks after your welfare and well-being. It is important to make use of this definition and make it handy in this precarious time when some mischievous elements will want to embrace you into their folds in the name of sectionalism, religious or tribal sentiments; to use and dump you in time to come.

I will advise you today to create your own definition of brotherhood in a way that suit your upward movement and growth in a favourable way; always expand your definition beyond the conjunction of blood relationship. Anybody that uses you to enrich himself, and later dump you is nothing but a foe. These are the kind of political friends we have been parading since Nigerian Independence more than fifty years ago. Their religious and tribal affiliation to their pawns has been that of affliction; look through to see for yourself.

The test of their 'good' leadership performance over the years can be seen in their level of impact in areas such as: infrastructural development, economy, good governance, poverty reduction, low corruption index and the increasing peace and unity of the nation. Unfortunately, we are dove-diving into a labyrinth through their subversive definition of brotherhood.

If your assessment has been a negative on their scorecards, it then means the old sectional patterns of choosing leaders from one section against competence should be discontinued for a superior process by hinging on performance and capability. Be truly a good judge, if your leaders have made your days and had successfully given you a swell beautiful and sustainable quality life then you can continue in the old fashion.

Those who deceive you into an unholy fraternity are your greatest enemy because they have not your interests at heart. If you are important to them, then the harvest and dividend of our nation should flow to your end as a citizen without having to struggle for benefits that are part of your fundamental rights.

It is not a good leadership delivery when the common man from the hinterland cannot aspire to become fully expressive because the benefits have to be divided through some untoward means. If you have been like many that have not been fairly treated it is time to bluff the old fashion brotherhood as you strive to attain better life and living condition without their deceptive alliance.

If you think you could have a better life here in Nigeria you are right. If you think good leadership is possible you are right. If you think you can build your own fortune here in Nigeria and have the comfort you have ever dreamt, of you are right. Whatever good thing you can imagine to take place in your life even here in Nigeria is possible.

You can have that great experience of living if you will today leave the deceptive divide of false brotherhood, zoning and sectionalism as you embrace the search for credible candidates for our leadership dream of one who does not necessarily have to be from your ethnic or tribal group – he is the man that will fulfill the dreams of our common greatness; he is the man sent from God. Today, let us leave all sentiments as we embrace the man who has the true heart to move things forward.

Doing things in certain ways, being principle driven in choosing leaders is the one fundamental way of building a buoyant nation.

Removing the Divides

To you my very dear brother from that distant corner of the country, may I ask you this question: Does it really matter where a leader comes from as much as the program he has for the common people; and of what pride is a no-do-well, corrupt politician from your zone? A society that will be great does not celebrate failure whether in school, job, politics or government. It is a disgrace to have a kinsman assume office he lacks ability to handle, worse still, he is inadequately prepare for.

A Yoruba adage goes: Omo wa ni, e je o se which means: He is our son, let him do it. This is our general cultural default in Africa as a whole and it tells a whole lot why we are where we are now – in lack an poverty.

Permit me to yet indulge you in this Yoruba adage for emphasis: Omo goo eni ko ti ma ku – ki ni'o pa omo naa bi'se ago. This one says: a child is foolish but the parents say it doesn't matter only if he doesn't die. The response in the proverb is kilo pa omo bi ago. What kills like folly? This relates to you and me: a foolish and incompetent leader will do you no good even if he is your kinsman; while a wise leader from the farthest part of Nigeria will benefit you even the more. The call here is to the wise hearted people of our noble country to stop celebrating mediocrity and failure; henceforth, let it be that whoever would take the reins of office should be credible and competent - it doesn't matter where the person comes from.

Bad leadership choice done by hitching for family, ethnic, tribe or zone will not get anyone far; at least it is incapable of sustaining both the power holder and his lieutenants for too long. At the end of the day, it will hurt the collaborators the most. A good illustration in not too distant time in the past is Samuel Doe of Liberia who upon attaining unto power destroyed virtually all his collaborators and allies that got him to power.

A more precise illustration is found in the Scripture. We have the story of Abimelech and the people of Shechem who were his blood relation from his mother's side. The people of Shechem and Abimelech collaborated, killed every other sons of his father from other wives except one son who escaped. After the massacre, they installed Abimelech their kinsman as the new leader of Israel. Within a short while (less than three years) the relationship went sour as Abimelech became offensive and oppressive to his own very people that got him into power, and the people of Shechem went into rebellion. Abimelech became too strong for them as he made a killing spree of the Shechemites and burnt a good number of his very dear people that made him king. He also died miserably in the struggle and rebellion. They were all collaborators in their common destruction.

The relevance of this true illustration is that if we choose our leaders based on tribal sentiments without consideration for credibility, such leaders will turn again later and cause our very own destruction directly or shortchanging us through weak leadership impact – evil leadership burn like fire. In Nigeria we should stop putting Abimelechs into leadership lines. Nigeria is where it is now because of this same culture of wanting to put our person in power even when we see him evidently lacking in credibility; Abimelech kind of leaders would do no one any good. He who has an ear let him hear.

Chapter Seven

THE BIG DIRTY GAMES

A major misconception of power is the thought that power is far away from us and that it is somewhere in government, politics or with some rich godfathers. In reality, power is with each and every one of us and it is what we do with the power in us that will determine how fast we will arrive at our Promised Land. It is the collective power of every one of us in a society or nation that the great rulers of the world make use of. Power could be given freely as in a free and fair election, stolen through rigging and electoral malpractices and by sheer use of brute force and military might. Generally, power starts with individuals; it is collective power that forms the government.

As citizens, our responsibility is to protect our individual power and when we want to give it out as a trust, it should be done willfully and freely and to such leaders who will protect our interests and welfares. One of the ways you exercise your power is through your votes. Never allow anyone to sell the lie to you that your vote doesn't count. Evil usurpers who call themselves leaders want you to believe this but it is both your civic and moral responsibility to make your vote count when you show up to exercise it. When everybody takes seriously the electoral process, like drops of water, they will build up to usher in a new dawn for the populace; when everybody chooses to believe that their votes count.

Sometimes, many of us cry foul about those bad leaders roaming the corridors of power. We claim we didn't elect them; but directly or indirectly, all leaders are allowed to be in place when we accept them as they are. If you refuse to go out and exercise your franchise, then you are increasingly making it difficult for credible leaders to come to office in the country. If you will not vote, you have no right to ask for good governance; more so, you have abused and belittled the power you have. Often, negligence and I-don't-care-attitude is the problem that makes us keep recycling bad leaders in government.

Since the power of our leaders are our collective power freely given out in trust, stolen or usurped: we should learn to guard our power to vote and also guard our rights; and whenever it is stolen, we should wrestle and get it back as reflected in June 12, 1993 election annulled by General Ibrahim Babangida.

Anytime you fail to vote, you make corrupt leaders happy but when you vote you reduce their chances, they are therefore not happy. This is also one of the reasons why bad leaders threaten or create violence to scare people away thus making it easy to rig or manipulate figures.

Each man has a unique and personal power through his vote, and by it has the power of expression which ought not to be wasted by any means. Therefore, never give out your vote carelessly to someone you cannot trust. Indeed, your vote is your life and your future in your country.

Look for men of character and to this give your vote: in this way you will be investing into your future and that of your children. Don't sell your votes and don't give it lightly. Stop! Don't sell your votes anymore for cups of rice, beans, garri, kerosene, oil or money. Selling your rights will always attract negative consequences and hardships - sooner or later.

When next we go to the polling booth to cast our votes, let us bear the story of Esau and Jacob his brother in our memory. Esau has enough excuse of great hunger, yes he justified why he has to get food for his stomach at the cost of his birthright. The Scripture tells us that later in life he wept with much tears to regain it but it was late. No matter what happens, give no one the privilege to deceptively steal your voting right. No reason is good enough for you to sell your vote; your excuse is only good enough for you. Be wise.

Be involved in deciding those who lead you by using this index: always go for a leader that has equitable interests of the citizens at heart: if he will not sell others to you, he will likewise not sell you to others.

We have considered the story of Esau, when he needs the satisfaction that comes from ones birthright he could not get it back; it was gone forever. The same thing happens when we allow some vain elements come around to steal our votes through deception. They use words and corruption as tools to sway you to treat your votes lightly thinking you are simple and light as wool, well, prove them wrong this once; esteem your votes please. Esau carelessly despised his birthrights and he paid dearly for it – his costly mistake is for our own learning.

Begin to observe how you treat your voting right. Your vote represents your character. If you are corrupt, then your vote has the tendency to be corrupted and by corruption it will be stolen. But I should trust that you are different as you join hands with a newly emerging generation of Nigerians of meaning who will vote rightly henceforth.

Beware of many of the politicians who are parading themselves around as economic and security messiahs; though they are with no good records to show yet they are busy jostling for lofty offices. The only thing they bank upon is their power to corrupt their way to the top. The season has to change.

We should be mindful of this fact: the means to winning an election is the same means to sustaining it. If you corrupt yourself to the top, you will sustain the system by corruption. We should not give means to politicians who seduce us to get our votes without justifiable merits. Remember: a corrupt leader is a dangerous being to parley with because he will devour that which is yours in due course.

Another group of concern is those citizens who see no reason to cast their votes. What such a person is saying is that he is lazy to make decision about his future and that he doesn't care about the welfare of his family and the future of his children and the unborn generation. He is saying that he is ready to accept anything presented to him by the society. He who has a vote and will not cast it is nothing but an undeserving weakling. The power of a vote well used is the power of advancement.

What we are saying expressly is this, in coming elections, let us as individuals do two things:

1.   Find credible candidate you can trust with your vote. In every election, there are always better candidates than the rest lot of politicians; they are such who have some elements of good character to advance the nation to the next level. Seek out such candidates.

2.   To this alone cast your votes without reservations or exchange with corrupt gifts. You don't need bribes or loaves of bread from questionable politicians before giving out your votes. A vote well cast is a vote for a better future. Therefore, cast your votes without fear or intimidation because every wrong vote cast will weigh against your future.

Anyone who gives you money in exchange for your vote is taking your future from you; don't be deceived!

The Costly Barter

Continuing on the above premise, most African nations give out their votes to the highest bidder (not absolutely right statement). Many of us don't give our votes willingly until we are offered something - stuff or money - in exchange. In advanced nations, aspirants seldom dole out money in exchange for votes (also not absolute for everyone and cases). Aspirants in the advance nations first of all belong to a party based on set of fundamental philosophy either democrat or labour, or republican and the likes. If they have the requisite merits, such candidates may win the trust of the people and their vote.

In advance societies, aspirants receive the supports of the voting public both morally and financially. This means that the citizens give in money or kind to facilitate the campaign process and progress of their preferred candidates thus the leaders owe the people. The reverse is usually the case in Nigeria where the aspirants are each taxed to give money to the voters. Although some have blamed poverty and lacks for this abysmal weakness of the mind in our system but not me, I see such low thinking to have sprung forth from poor value, poor foresight, corrupt tendency and greed.

What we need to do really is to come as a people for once and shun bribery as a yardstick for giving out votes. We should have the foresight and knowledge that a credible candidate will give us much better state of development; so there is no basis for asking him for a token of bribe before giving him the vote he needed to do good. By scrambling for crumbs of breads before giving a vote, we have nailed our rights to fair leadership to the tree of failure. If we learn the habit of delaying our gratification, we can easily see through as we cast our suffrage wisely; sometime if we want to get things right, we can go all the way to sponsor a credible candidate who is without the financial power by giving out our widow's mite. Come to think of it: If the millions of Nigerians will donate a hundred naira to fund the political career of a credible candidate then this would amount to enough money to ease the challenges of an emerging aspirant.

Think first of what you can give to make our politics better, think of what you can offer to help Nigeria begin to produce quality leaders. As long as we think of what we will get from the aspiring political class we would be blinded to see through. To rephrasing J.F. Kennedy, former American President: Think not of what the nation will do for you, think of what you will do for Nigeria. What this demands of us is that we should think firstly as givers. America learnt this, years ago through this ebullient president of theirs when our own democracy was just at infancy. That would have been the best time for us as a nation too to learn it, it should have been part of our narrative from the get go but it is not too late for us to learn it now.

The giving nations are the growing nations while the takers don't amount to anything. Poverty and underdevelopment are signs of selfish and greedy society; in such a society lots of the people are takers and not givers. This starts with whether we use our votes as means to give or take. Let each of us open our eyes and see what we can give towards the success of the upcoming elections and many more after it.

The best gift to a nation is for its citizens to find a credible candidate, canvass for votes and indeed vote him and further encourage fellow citizens to vote him; this is one of the most valuable contributions to nation building. The monies, food stuff and material things you collect can only last you a couple of days but good governance is a solid foundation that will serve us and the future generations

If we would give firstly our unreserved support to good candidacy then we can be hopeful for a great leadership outcome. A man you trusted into public office will be more careful to listen to you than the one who stole the votes through subversive manipulations. We can make things work out if we would follow the simple ideas above.

The True Measure of a Leader

Many would-be leaders make great speeches that could compare with those of Awolowo and Lincoln; it is a moment of flawless talk that could compare to those of Ige and Cicero.

Our leaders believe that you and I are easily fooled and unintelligent pack who they can deceive when they choose to. They believe we don't know our left from right so they come with great promises to transform our system for the better even when they have no track record of success or integrity whatsoever.

On this note, it is time we made this lip-serving people know that we are no longer given to mere words and empty promises. Our patience and enduring spirits should no longer be comfortable with mediocrity and non-performance as we begin to demand for character, integrity and discipline from our leaders. Talking about performance, some of these leaders are so woeful that we could hope for improvement from them if the case be that they underperformed; but no, under-performance is not even on the table, what they give us is outright non-performance and there is a world of difference. Those who lead our nation should be people with high moral standard and worthy models for the next generation. Leaders should be beyond reproach.

There was this case of former American president, Bill Clinton and Monica Lewinsky and it was a national issue. The big issue is that the president of the great nation cannot afford to lower his moral guard, condescending to the life of the "common": others may but not the esteemed their president. Until our leaders tower above the citizens morally, the nation will continue to nose-dive into the abyss of depreciation. Any nation that would be preeminent cannot but have leaders who tower above and serve as the moral compass for the entire society. Therefore, we need more men of moral value in our politics than ever, the leader must be better than the followers.

The morality of the leader has a high correlation with the development and advancement of the society. Watch out the advanced nations, you will observe that their leaders are mostly men of their words. Check out men like Mahatma Gandhi, Abraham Lincoln and Nelson Mandela, their character has a lot of bearing on their society. In Nigeria, we have not yet successfully produced such icon of international recognition in our politics or governance. The examples of men listed above are the men that charted new course for several generations into the future.

It is now ever so clearer to us that words alone do not position a nation on the path of greatness and that leadership is known, identified, described and assessed not only by words alone but also by character. Our impact is in proportion to our character. A man rises or falls to the level of his character. It is character that determines what a man will do under any given circumstance. A leader may deceive us to get to power but he will need character to sell himself in the heart of the people. Power may be won through subversive means but character will create a lasting legacy you will leave behind. The great men who made history are sustained in our memory not as a result of their power or great words but because of their consistency in character.

To the electorate, we should become very careful in the face of sugar-coated tongues of our politicians who are determined to sway us aside by their sweet tongue. The simple test of the quality of the leader you choose is in their character; for a tree is known by the kind of fruits it bears. An evil genius with the voice of an angel will yield no better program in his domain except those with devilish signature all over it. A leopard cannot change its skin. Character is the real man. This is why the true person behind the sweet words and promises will in matter of time reveal his true identity because no one can give what he doesn't have. A leader with a loose moral standing, broken home and assembly of other vices cannot transform overnight into a messiah even if he speaks eloquently like an angel.

In the light of the above, let us always be careful to study and research into those whom we set to govern us. We will do good to always painstakingly ask for records, performance and personal ideology of supposed candidates. After this, let us ask after their political ideology and programs as individual politicians. If we take our time to know the type of people wanting to rule us we will begin to have quality leadership in our rein.

As a leader is so is his performance.

Political Entrepreneurs, Self-Serving Elders and the People

It is time we direct our discussion to our elders; the self-serving elders and the political entrepreneurs who have been living off on the juice of this nation's wealth.

Let us take a look at the political entrepreneurs of our estate. Political entrepreneurs are group of politicians whose primary aim in leadership is to convert public funds to self-enrichment. Their sole purpose is to swell their purse by stealing and converting public funds for personal use; they mind every naira notes and ensure that only projects that help them become richer see the light of the day. The welfare of their followers is secondary and this is why projects that have the tendency to make them richer are often given preferences. Their sole purpose in leadership is to fleece the society, plunder its wealth and make merchandise of the public trust. They are rich but outside government position they grow financially lean because they don't know how to make their own money without the government. This is why they would do just anything to be in the ruling group. Outside politics they are like fish out of the water.

Another group is the self-serving elders: statesmen, religious leaders, eminent personalities and traditional heads and chiefs who for the sake of cheap popularity, gifts, and money team up with the corrupt leaders in government to drain off the wealth of the society through collaborative greed. Example is our religious leaders who are content to be identified with just any crop of leaders so far they are given part of the stolen loots as 'gifts' from the top. Traditional leaders are not left out of the game as they jostle for whatever they can make as gain from the government of the day even when the fundamental rights of their followers are being denied or abused; so do many of the supposed statesmen who are often pseudo-godfathers. For this latter group use their influence to further bring the populace into servitude. They have gone out to abuse their trust with bribes from the top.

The true essence of the religious leaders, traditional chiefs and the elders is to serve as both guard and guide of the welfare of their subject. They ought to be the watchmen against anti-people policies and programs.

The above discussion calls for reflection by various stakeholders to pitch camp away from the corrupt politicians else their dishonourable partnership will lead them into disgraceful ends; it is only a matter of time.

Leaders who fleece their followers are only helping in self destruction. Such a person is only busy defacing all the legacies that took him up and gradually creating an inglorious exit. Leadership is trust which last for a limited time (even a lifetime is limited in itself), if the trust is used well to serve the interests of the subjects it becomes the gateway of becoming immortalized; but if it is used to serve personal interests such a leader would have his name written on water.

If we care to know, history has interest in the preservation of the names of only leaders who served the people with memorials built for them. On the other hand, self serving leaders never worth a pinch of salt as they have their legacy corrupted while alive. This is why many years later; some leaders stand out as colossus while others are reduced into specs in history.

Towing The Path Of Nonviolence

Nonviolence is the emerging alternative for settling differences based on the power of truth and love by using dialogues and peaceful demonstration. Great leaders opt in for nonviolent means to settle disputes while ruthless ones go violent; so it applies to individuals and citizens. Superior warfare tactic is to stop war before it ever started or issues get degenerated (saying same thing in different words), while ordinary folks vent their full anger but seek recourse only after the full cycle of mayhem and war had been completed.

If you are for truth and love, you will avoid violence by all means by seeking equity and justice not minding which side of the divide you find yourself. Abraham Lincoln was on the stronger side of the divide being a white man, but the strong impressions on his conscience for equity and justice led him to free the slaves and abolish slavery in America. It was not the popular opinion then but history has vindicated him and generations after salute his courage to do the right thing.

Violence is an offshoot of irrepressible hatred for others. If you can find love within you will not want anyone hurt as you press for what is due you. On this note, I will like to state that violence as a nature is the manifestation of the lower man which seeks for the interest of certain individuals or groups at the expense of others. Such irrepressible hatred was what led to Adolf Hitler's mass murder of the Jews spurned through his Nazi regime (The Third Reich).

Violence in whatever form destroys and damages the existing good structure on which a society is built. Wildness is not the way of the advance man and anyone seeking for expression by violence is only bowing to his animal nature and not to his superior form. The truth is: violence in all its form is a cover up for weakness and not strength; strong people don't destroy instead they build and make the world a better place for all.

If we all understand that we are all brothers and sisters here on earth we would refrain from violence – everyman is related to every other person somewhere down the genealogy line. Thus if some weak politicians from nowhere is trying to create divides let us rise up and tell them we are brothers and sisters. So we should begin to celebrate each other and not be too careful from what section a leader comes from. What we need is brotherliness in nationhood.

No matter the perceived differences, the absolute truth is that we are brothers somewhere down the line. No matter the grievances we may have, love would overlook offences and seek for constructive means for settlement because brothers will sometime offend each other and still find a way to come together.

Whosoever intends to recruit you as tool for violence has none of your interest at heart. If you have somebody like that around you, tell them to go and recruit their own children, siblings and parents; let those carry the guns, cutlasses, knives and armaments. If their family members are too sophisticated to engage in such brutality then you should know that they hate you and are daredevil masters. Tell them you are also too sophisticated for violence; slaves are sent out in the night to carry out odd jobs; you are an honourable citizen.

The reality is that the evil geniuses of our primitive politics don't ask their blood relation to lead the violence they created. Those who engage you in violent escapades don't see you as their brother but a tool to be used and dumped. You must be a big fool to think that you are loved by these miscreants in politics and government because they offer you money when sent on violent suicidal mission. Such a leader has nothing to lose if you die, this is why he will shield his family but expose you.

Those who seek for peace across the divides are those who really have the cord of brotherhood; find such, melt your differences and find common goals to pursue.

One good reason why violence should be eschewed in our nation is this: we should see ourselves as highly exalted citizens and not common slaves; don't make yourself a slave because someone is pushing you on the brink of old fashion ideology of hate. Come up higher, you are a citizen of a great nation, the biggest nation in the heart of Africa, the emerging pride of Africa. To be divided is to grow weaker and smaller. Let us drop those things that divide us; we are one.

Note: We can inculcate art (music and movies) as a means to propagate preferred ideology. We should find a way to use the instrumentality of art to sell the newer truth of love and peace. People like Angelique Kidjo sang We Are One, Onyeka Owenu sang One Love Brings Us Together etc. other artists and film makers should follow suit and contribute to the labour of our heroes past.

Mahatma Gandhi (Hindu) of India, Bishop Desmond Tutu and Nelson Mandela of South Africa were examples of men that promoted peace in their nations in times of crisis.

Let men and women from Sokoto to Lagos, Aba to Ibadan, Calabar to Jos and to Bauchi drop their weapons of hate as we embrace one another in brotherliness in spite of diversity of religion, tribe, ethnicity or other perceived diversity. This can only be the basis for an emerging great nation and economy.

Chapter Eight

SHIFT FOR A SUSTAINABLE
MODEL OF CHANGE

The Achilles' heel of most leaders is what they perceive about the led. This is the foundation of leaders' downfall: when their perceptions about why they are there is wrong, every other thing will go wrong.

Government and its leadership representatives are around primarily to organize, administrate, and coordinate resources which include human capital. They are not called to lord over or force upon the citizens their ideology.

The resources – especially the human capital - are already in place, the leader is to organize and coordinate them to productive end. In organizing, you position the resources to rightly suit its purpose and place, in the same way you organize your home wares and appliances; what should be in the living room should not be taken into the bedroom. In coordinating resources you direct them for right use.

Narrowing down resources to human, effective leader administers, organizes and coordinates his people to optimize their contribution and usefulness to themselves and the organization. Leaders fail when they lose sight of these three responsibilities: administration, organization and coordination. Most leaders lose sight of these vital responsibilities from the beginning for some reasons. Firstly, they undermine the power of the citizens to create the good, and that within the people lay the power to change.

A big blunder subsists when a leader believes that he is the one bringing changes to the led. This is untrue, the change you want, the development, the grand society is within the people, and the leader's role is to create harmony from the noise of uncoordinated expression of the citizens. Ignorance of what leadership and governance means has rendered many of our officials clueless in their appointments. They are not to create life for the people; instead they are to bring out the expression of the life in the people.

Authority is only useful to the extent that it gives individuals opportunity for development, expression, enlargement and pursuit of his life's goals. To create less life for the citizens is an aberration stemming out of ignorance and in making the people better, you make the nation better.

Extolling and enhancing the expression of the good in citizens is the pathway to national development. Leaders should know that there is latent capability within each citizen to do good, grow and expand. What citizens need is amenable conditions that will aid their flourishing to amplify right doing or vices. So if the government is supportive of the good, good will multiply in due season.

No matter how good the intention of a leader is, no matter how much good he gave, if he does not involve and employ the citizens' interests it will be a flash in the pan. Sustainable good is one in which the people are part of a program from the conceptualization stage through the various growth stages and to the very end of implementation.

The second reason for lack of sustainability of change program is related to abuse of power. In this wise the leader tend to live above the law, do as he pleases, careless and lacking in moral scruple; yet expect a process of change to sail through. The leader should always understand that within the citizens lies the ultimate power for change; yet the initial model to catalyze the much needed transformation is the lifestyle of the leader.

Within the ambit of abuse of power is autocratic use of authority to influence decisions and change. Since such changes are forced, they will last only as long as the leader is within range. Changes that are sustained are those that speak to the hearts of the citizens and which elicit their participation.

Power is best used when it is administered to help followers realize a constructive alternative of benefits, and force to be used only when certain citizens begin to act in ways that are injurious to fair dealings and the common good.

The third reason for lack of sustainability of change and good governance is the inherent culture of governance in a nation or society. For instance, in Nigeria there is seldom continuity of programs and policies from one regime or government to another. This lack of continuity has led to the death of vibrant projects which are often replaced by inferior ones. A new leader could arise and jealously kill a program because it did not start with him, this is alarming and barbaric.

Policy, program or project should not be sustained or killed based on who projected it: an idea should be sustained once it brings much benefit to the citizens.

Another side to culture of governance is bedeviled by sentimental successor programs where the less qualified to sustain a growing economy, policy or program is appointed to take over from a predecessor to satisfy some sentimental obligations. Therefore, there is rarely a guarantee for an effective successor plan for continuity or sustainability of a program or policy in our public places. This is a big hurdle to cross if Nigeria would ever know greatness.

The fourth factor that impinges on sustainability of virile project is leader's myopic orientation that the citizens are low class, inferior and lacking in adequate knowledge to move the state forward; therefore, no consultation or inclusion of the ideas or ideologies of the citizens in major decisions. The leader who will succeed in the long haul needs to be abreast of this truth that everyone is important and with certain depth of knowledge and flavor of ability to inject into a system.

You can never undermine the ingenuity of the citizens of the world when they are given the wings to fly. Consult the mind of the citizens and you will be amazed how they would help bring life to the concept at hand: leverage on their knowledge, wisdom and know-how – this should include the local peasants. A peasant in a locality will probably have certain depth of knowledge of his culture and environment than a professor!

Everyone has his own unique area of endowment and expertise as each of us in a certain capacity is a custodian of some specific knowledge.

The Bottom-up Change

The problem of governance and leadership can never be dealt with without such a reprogramming, education and campaigns targeting the citizens; this is based on the understanding that the leaders are products of the citizens. To raise great leaders we must firstly raise great citizens and to have exceptional leadership is to build exceptional citizens. The emerging new leaders were once on equal status as the next citizen. So to get the leadership system right we need to get the acts of citizenship right. We have been looking upward for so long but are yet to have respite or solution to the economic or leadership impasse we are so far dipped in. The answer to national growth lies right in the power and participation of the people.

Over the years we have always believed and wish a leader would come on stage and apply his magic wand to achieve a fast transformation of the society without significant input of the citizens. This is not possible.

Top-down solution will seldom bring the desirable succor to the poverty and lack of the citizens.

Why leaders alone cannot make much difference is this: The leaders and followers are both cast out of the same social and environmental molds. Also, average leader will tend to enhance what the community chose as acceptable; tending not to rock the boat. Followers with the wrong mind set cannot be so easily led on the path of change until their thinking is affected. Therefore, there would have to be a deep level of cooperation between the leaders and the led to make changes.

On this premise, the main work of a leader is to convert the hearts of the followers to be on the same plane such that they could work together to achieve common goals. Thus, the hardest and most important work of a leader is to transform the hearts of the followers to journey with him to where they ought to go and not where they want. When the heart is affected the citizens are no longer acting as zombie but as critical stakeholders.

Most leaders look for the quickest means: create a policy, back it up with legislation and driven by the law enforcement agents, do this for a while and get grinded because of the oppositions.

This is what we call top-down design: create a program by a few suggested egg-heads and erudite scholars, and then force it down on the rest for compliance. It is a quick means but certainly set to fail. A program that would succeed needs to pass through proper consultation, communication and feedback with the base, that is, the citizens because they constitute the bulk of the society. Furthermore, it makes sense to start any planning with the citizens because at the end of the day, the greater part of policies and programs are geared towards them; so it is important to put them in the big picture and give them active roles to play.

Any leader that wants to do greatly must observe that he gives premium respect and recognition to the citizens, and ask for their participation and involvement from time to time. The crudest of persons when refined is full of ingenuity and a role to play to bring into place the desired outcome.

In warfare, every hand recruited is a potential plus to winning a battle. Therefore, one needs to sell the picture of transformation in a way that it will elicit participation of most citizens without applying any negative inducement. Every citizen won to your side is a plus.

Bottom-up change does not mean leaving the citizens to run any idea without control. We need to understand fundamentally that citizens are like build-up of mass of water which if not properly channeled will wreck the environment. Citizens are to be checked and controlled as you would a dam. Although, the leader is not called to carry the burden of the citizens unduly, yet his duty is to create the channel of flow to make the citizens take responsibilities of creating the change they want; let each citizen bear his own share of national responsibilities.

Leaders create the channel through which the citizens flow. The work of the leader is not to create changes alone. His primary work is to create or offer models to serve as blueprints for the citizens to work upon. The citizen should make the changes together.

Looking intently into the above paragraph, we could easily find out why many leaders are underperforming. They are trying to do what the citizens should do, since they are engrossed in activities and 'poverty alleviation schemes or 7 point transformation agenda' as they commonly call it, they could not see reason to present a working blueprint to the people. They overestimate their own strength and underestimate that of the citizens; doing this, they shot themselves at the heel and advancement becomes impossible. Leadership is about knowing what to do and assigning, delegating or allowing others to do what only they can do.

It may look like a short-cut when you chose to run a top-down government but taking a closer look, it is overly expensive. Using a simple illustration, which one is cheaper of these two; to run a campaign with hundreds of participation and supporters to carry the campaign down to their community or spend huge sum on media campaign? Experience has shown that you will get better result when you have excited people supporting your cause than media presence. The media is like the faceless top-down approach of government, it does not make deep penetration like having the human side (the interpersonal and one-to-one type) to impact. The citizens are human faces you need for development, change and transformation.

Top-down program is an expensive option, short-live and for a short-term agenda. Bottom-up is less expensive when weighed along with the overall output and to be utilized when you desire a long-term result. The bottom-up process engages the citizens in the process of change

Chapter Nine

THE MESSAGE

There are three important parts that lead to change in a society: value, perception and re-branding. It is rather unfortunate that subsequent government leaders have always settled for the quick fix alternative without firstly addressing the value system and perception of the citizens they create slogans and propaganda and these they tagged their re-branding projects.

It is either these leaders are ignorant of what it takes, which I doubt because they are surrounded by well educated advisers and consultants or they are paying mere lip service. I want to believe that many of the leaders we have are out to deceive the people. So they choose the easy alternative. Hyping slogans and jingles are not enough to make a people drop their old culture for a new one. If a new value and perception are not put in place, no re-branding can be achieved.

Value Shift, the Way Out

Value shift is the means to enduring change while re-branding is the end. Re-branding has a process that must be followed. The re-branding is like a harvest while value shift is the real work. Many politicians and leaders run away from the real work. Value change will affect everyone and require the commitment of everybody starting with the leaders' choices and lifestyle.

Often, leaders want changes but they are not ready to make their own personal sacrifices.

Years ago, some of our national leaders advocated the purchase of made-in-Nigeria goods but they could not enforce or win the loyalty of the citizens to do this because they were worst culprit who indulge to excess the use of imported goods.

At another time leaders in government wanted to cut costs of governance, they deem it fit to start with cutting the remuneration of civil servants but met brick walls because the citizens saw insincere government leaders. Each of the leaders earns hundred times what each civil servant is earning but could not lead by exemplary sacrifice of their own comforts.

Many times, we do not see meaningful change largely due to the insincerity of our leaders and their lack of commitment and sacrifice. A lip-service change is a mere propaganda which is created as time fillers.

Real change is tasking and demanding; it requires overhauling of old habits, cultures, ways of life and thinking.

Even though we like to talk about change, it is often mere talk. Average human beings are not so patient enough to endure the process of change; so is ready to fight the change he desires when it is non-achievable within reasonable boundary of time. The fear, uncertainty and the newness will often make us to want to settle for the old small life.

It takes a bold and courageous leader to confront the old style and value and win support gradually until the people are willing to adopt the new value through new perception which can only yield after much awareness, advocacy and reorientation. A true leader who loves the people indeed will not give up half-way out but will go the full length until the new rewarding lifestyle is attained; then and only then can we say a re-branding has been achieved.

The work of the leader is to showcase the new values he wanted to be adopted using every medium and platform that could help. Value is more than a campaign slogan; it has an intrinsic lifestyle that should go with it.

According to Oxford English dictionary values can be defined as belief about what is right and wrong and what is important in life which relates to cultural, social and moral values.

That a society holds on to certain values does not make them right. It is the outcome of those beliefs that matters. The work of a leader is to shift the people to embrace new and specific values which would be of benefit.

The role of a slogan is to rally the people to adopt the new values. If a slogan points nowhere, it becomes useless, ineffective and a mere propaganda tool. The work of the slogan and other campaign tools is to reinforce the adoption of the new positive values.

The end is to change the perception of the citizens; perception as to what is right or wrong. Perception change is important. Someone may literally know that smokers are liable to die young, yet may have a different perception that supports his smoking habit.

Average Nigerian knows that corruption is bad, but average Nigerian indulge in it. The perception is faulty: everyone wants to quickly amass wealth, steal public funds, and divert public goods for personal use. Everyone believes that corruption will affect the general well being of the nation, but no one wants to agree that his own contribution to corruption makes much a difference. We have forgotten that little drops of water make the mighty ocean! We need to understand that a nation's economy is the accumulation of the citizen's actions and inactions without leaving anybody out. Peace is achieved when everybody chose to be at peace with each other.

One man cannot steal the fund of an entire nation, one man cannot create war, one man cannot rule oppressively and one man cannot run a system without others. Beneath the leaders are hundreds and thousands of citizens as collaborators. The leader holds sway for as long as he has citizens who actively or passively give him the support he needs.

Many times we see the leader emptying a nation's treasury, but with closer look you see millions of his kind around the corner like vultures lurking around a corpse, waiting for their own turn. Such evil leader only chose to use few of these vultures to perfect his looting.

A society whose value system entrenches transparency, probity and accountability will quickly corner a greedy leader. A leader is often a reflection of the people. If the people of a nation have different values they will soon push out a leader with divergent values whether good or bad.

Raising Change Leaders

When a leader wants to transform a society, he needs to find a way of communicating his ideals with relevant stakeholders and with the hope of raising a strong team. To go from door-to-door alone trying to effect the change is to undertake an impossible journey that ends nowhere.

A change crusader must raise or have his change team. His team would be anticipated to become the change leaders: people with direct relationships with him. Change leaders are best chosen out among the people who are already in leadership position because they already have power of influence on certain individuals. With a well communicated statement of change, these leaders can reach out to hundreds, thousands and even millions at a time.

Conversely, you can also adopt among your team of change leaders, people who exhibit great leadership potential reaching them through various media, and doing your selections through identifiable traits such as passion, potential, experience etc.

Overall, one change leader would be empowered to affect other people who also go ahead to affect others. This is what a boomerang looks like. Before long the much awaited change will boomerang, and the change we want will therefore become everybody's change.

A good point to begin is raising your first change team by firstly creating reorientation and reordering of their value system. Once this is successfully done; to be confirmed, use a test indices or create a key performance indicator, then marshal the team for grass-root mobilization for hundreds, thousands and millions to identify with you using a holistic process, border-to-border technique; ensuring engagement and accountability across board and all the way!

The Biggest Denominator

The biggest denominator to an effective branding or change programme is the message. The message should elicit interest, be attractive, and desirable enough to provoke a course of action.

A message that would attract the average person out there should be woven around the individual; it should be personalized. Let each person see himself at the centre of events, he will be ready to protect it. Make it other people's thing and he will not be serious about it.

Take a look at parents; they go the extra mile to fend for their own children but to a lesser degree when it is about other people's children: this is not a vice but a demonstration of human nature which tends to protect what is personalized in their name.

Again take a look at our names. We get so attached to our names that we respond by innate reflex wherever it is mentioned.

We can so much build a change program that people will naturally respond to by reflex action, through an automatic movement towards the change.

This means that if you want a large participation, create a clarion call that gives the individual in the big ship of the nation a bit of the action. Let everyone be involved, active, responsible to and to contribute to the big vision and this should be captured in the message; a message that should be inclusive.

An analytical study why previous national re-branding campaigns failed can be seen quickly in their messages — messages that are not inclusive.

Some of the past Rebranding Change Projects

Ethical Revolution   — Alhaji Shehu Shagari era (1979-1983)

War Against Indiscipline (WAI)– General Mohammadu Buhari (1984)

Mass Mobilization for Social Justice, Self-reliance and Economic Recovery (MAMSER) – General Ibrahim Babangida Era (1985-1993)

War Against Indiscipline and Corruption (WAIC) – General Sani Abacha (1994)

Heart of Africa Foundation   — Olusegun Obasanjo

Good People, Great Nation   — Dora Akunyili (2009)

I will make reference to just two of the above projects because most of them hardly made any significant impression.

The first I will be referring to was War Against Indiscipline (WAI) by General Mohammadu Buhari (1984). It was deemed to be the most laudable based on general opinion. Its alibi was that it was driven on the wing of military force; compliance was out of fear and not out of deep conviction, devotion or change of value. Therefore, people comply as long as the government was in power. Secondly, the succeeding government of Ibrahim Babangida took over through coup, so he has to jettison most programs of Buhari administration which WAI was included. Average Nigerian had a sigh of relief from WAI, the discipline and compliance attached became a strong point through which Babangida subverted the hearts of the people to his own government. WAI went through the stretch for as long as the government was in power because it was not mobilized through the people's power.

History remained that it was the closest thing to a meaningful change, the main problem was that the citizens were not in the big picture of the drive: the citizens were on the sideline as the military drove it.

The other re-branding project worth mentioning was that established by Dora Akunyili of blessed memory who was then the Minister of Information. It was tagged: Good People, Great Nation. It has the flavor of the people, the citizen opened their hands to embrace it but suddenly the momentum died from the government's side and the vision was not sustained!

Good people, Great Nation: A message with deep meaning. It implied that Nigerian people are inherently good, capable of doing good and are good; and these good people make a great nation, and would make the nation much greater!

'Good people' is a collective statement but lack the power to elicit active participation of the individual person. Everybody's thing is nobody's thing. 'Good People' is collective but not inclusive. We need a message that will create a clarion call from the individual - an inclusive message.

On this premise, here is a statement posited to Dr. Kayode Fayemi delivered in a speech at the 2013 Verdant Zeal Innovation Lecture series. Kayode Fayemi traced the failure of efforts at re-branding Nigeria to "lack of value and the inability of successive administrations to articulate a strategic national vision and attune institutional realities to match the vision".

Source: http://www.newstrack.ng/business/economy/7044-can-buhari-rebranding-nigeria

If you take a look at his statement, the words "lack of value" stands out in the sentence. Many of those who often shoulder themselves with the responsibility of national re-branding exercises in Nigeria have questionable characters and are people of low moral pedigree.

The second thought is the inability to articulate a strategic national vision. A worthwhile re-branding program should wear a national look. A national look does not necessarily mean government-driven but that it should be embraced by the citizens on national scale and beyond its national outlook is the need to apply a tested framework or a creative design and to bring to bear the institutional realities of what would work for Nigeria. In other words, it should not be a borrowed concept from another country but indigenously customized to face the reality confronting us based on our ethnic diversity, beliefs, religions and values. In this wise, I am not against the use of a globally tested models, adaptation or frameworks that works; but we should refrain from replication and copying an exact concept and transplanting it on our national soil. No two countries are exactly or empirically the same.

Again, most of the previous government re-branding exercises lack one or both of the following:

They are not community based or community driven: somebody high up at the federal capital concoct a program and send it to be implemented at the community level. Things don't work that way. The communities have to be carried along, well represented and included for thorough in-reaching and participation.

The program has no deliberate blueprints for communities from one era, government or generation to the next. Most re-branding concept in this country has no depth in reaching the people and also do not have future elements which let it away as possibly mere propaganda tool for a specific government and for a time.

From the above discussion, we could deduce why re-branding projects fail and below we have what should not be done:

It should not be leaders owned pet project. So far pet projects are ran by successive governments' personnel to last as long as they are in power. Let it not be the president's affairs but the peoples.

Presidential programs will be short of life and at the end of the day waste of state resources while people's programs will endure.

Also, government should not take ownership of the change project. The government should see herself as the midwife of change which the citizens want to give birth to.

Most adults can read between lines whether a project is set up for genuine reasons or for propaganda sake. Once they see it as a propaganda tool they will lose interest quickly, waiting until they can see a genuine project to embrace.

A change brand that would become sustainable cannot be self seeking, deceptive or laden with ulterior motives. You shouldn't promote your sentiments as a brand project. You will be doing the nation wrong to want to promote religious or tribal cause as a national identity. What is good for the goose is good for the gander; when using the national platforms, content designed should be mutually beneficial. This I believe to be godly in all ramifications.

Change brand should be equally disposed to all classes not just for one side of the divide. For instance: The Good People, Great Nation project launched by Dora Akunyili was more an elite disposed program, it was never felt at the grass-root. As it runs in the city, it should be felt in our slums and villages. It should be a clarion call for all.

Melting the Divide

A change message for national re-branding should be inclusive; personalized and directed to all. It should be inclusive: everyone should have a role to play whether great or small and each person's contribution should be unique, that is personalized and distinct. Yoking people to play the same role is anathema to life and would be boring and it will suffer discontinuity. Take drama acting as case study. If everyone has to act the same role nobody will take his time to watch it; variety is the spice of life. Individuals should be allowed to contribute to the growth of the nation according to his ability and interest.

The real change we need requires that each of us is represented in it, inclusive and personalized. The gain should be apportioned with probity and equity according to ones contribution, thus gain directed to all and sundry.

Man is made to profit, yet it becomes a vice and shrewd to make gains where one has not laboured, conversely it is an evil under the heaven to labour and not be given the privilege to benefit from it. A healthy system is one in which individual is given a level playing field to make profit whether in cash, kind or otherwise from his input to life.

On this premise, people would be drawn to programs and opportunities that promise fair return and which increase them and that which makes life better and offer fulfillment or satisfaction. Man is made for advancement. When you want men to share in a message, let them see where it is taking them and when the distribution of benefit is in your charge, be truthful to the promise with sincerity, fair play and equity.

A national re-branding program should offer equal opportunity for all. When a re-branding program is all inclusive, personalized, all involving and well directed to benefit all, it will elicit cross border participation. In this wise, it will stand out as every one's program; for the people and their common interest. The design may have a strong influence and backing from the government, yet it must not be seen as government own thing: instead, it should portray a design with benefit to all.

Let us not forget: Men gravitate toward benefit.

The Message Of Change

For the first time in our national history, we are coming close to creating an inclusive message in the change mantra. This is not a politically inspired message nor does it have any special political affiliation; I think. The reason is that my team has been running with a slogan tagged: "I Am the Change Nigeria Needs" a message of change that has been before any political class ever touted a change mantra.

I remembered vividly in the year 2009, I had a unique inspiration which became validated, with confirmations so to speak - through the impact it made.

I have viewed our national divides expanding and the chasm seems unassailable because each person and group point outside their domain as the source of our national woes. You see one tribe pointing to the other and one religion strives with another; this has no end. Until we take responsibility and allow change to begin with us, we are going nowhere; and the fact that the healing of these divides cannot be conjured by any one individual or group without involving you and me, and everyone else.

Nigeria problem is not caused by one person, not by a class or group. And as long as each of us failed to take responsibility, we will continue to remain and be where we are now, and we run the risk things even growing a whole lot worse.

I have interacted with the mind of our leaders: many of the good intentioned ones are frustrated because they thought the citizens are impatient and do lack perseverance. Leaders often believe that they failed because the citizens are not cooperating and supportive. Citizens should learn that they have a part to play: nothing good comes cheap; there is a price to be paid for every fortune in life. The majority of the citizens don't want to pay the price yet they want the prize of a quality life. You cannot eat your cake and have it. Leaders alone cannot do the magic!

Many of the citizens don't really know what they want and the magnitude of the price they have to pay. This is why it is easy for ill intentioned politicians to manipulate them with a promise to give the citizens a fair haven for a price of nothing. Most citizens' frame of mind is to follow an imaginary stress free life where government does everything. Leaders believe that the citizens can easily be bought because they are unstable in their wants, desires and expectations; all which they expect to come from the little gods of politics and government.

The citizens on the other side of the divide believe that the leaders are the culprits and villains of our national woes. But on critical assessment both the government which represents the leaders and the citizens are collaborators and are responsible for where the country is.

In the same way, the diverse religious groups and their leaders are not excluded. The religious and moral cultures of a society are strong indices to the growth of a nation. Religion should hitherto serve as a vehicle to move the country forward and not as basis for conflict and aggressive lifestyle that impedes on development.

The different ethnic and tribal blocs are containment of the citizens; if a society breeds corruption, watch the values that take preeminence. If every tribe and ethnic group makes up their minds to stand for that which is good, right, honest and fair, in no time the nation will be set for advancement.

In view of the above discussion, it is imperative that the citizens in their entirety determine the fate of a nation; not just the government, not just a religious group but every religion, and not just an ethnic or tribal group but everyone.

On this premise we have gotten to the point whereby we are no longer expected to wait for the government because the government in reality has no power of its own. Whatever power we feel inherent in the government is the life and meaning the citizens gave it. Government is a dummy without the citizens. This is the truth many of the government leaders will not want you to know. They will rather want to keep you uninformed so that you continue to think that "government is powerful", and so powerful to determine the fate of the citizens. Although this is not altogether false: government is as powerful as much as we want it to.

The unfortunate part of the matter is that in spite of the repository power of the citizens, the uninformed and non-knowledgeable citizens cannot deliver a progressive state. A perverted power is injurious and destructive; raw and unprocessed power is of no use: when citizens' power is perverted they serve as ready tools for terrorism, militancy, and political mercenaries.

The power that you do not acknowledge can be stolen from you. This is what "government" has done these past years; it steals the power that belongs to the people.

Any government that fails to acknowledge the inherent power in the citizens and help cultivate it is doomed to fail in a matter of time. When a government steals or usurps the power of the people it becomes a problem to growth, on the other hands the more a government liberates its people, empowers and gives them the wings to fly the more the state and nation flourishes.

Ronald Reagan in his inaugural speech reiterated the power of the citizens to build the nation of America through the wisdom of the founding fathers, and he said: "people keep looking to government for the answer and government is the problem". In other words: the government should be less "powerful" and the people made more powerful in order to create answers for governance.

In essence, Reagan is saying that the answer is not in the government but within the citizens and that the problem that makes us look toward the government is often caused by the government who dis-empowered us to look away from the power within each of us.

A Republican presidential aspirant Ben Carson in the U.S.A. 2016 elections also said it this way: "We've been conditioned to think that only politicians can solve our problems. But at some point, maybe we will wake up and recognize that it was politicians who created our problems".

Let us take a look at our home grown federal system and the constitution back here in Nigeria; they are filled with inequalities and prejudices. Somebody comes to power and leaning on his sentiments he favours a group and would go ahead and tweak the federal system and the constitution in favour of his sentiments, then another comes again and tilts things in the direction of his own interest. Those who were not given fair treatment by such intrigues would often create some levels of disturbances at their own end to register their grievances as they reek with resentment and anger because someone is cheating them; this often lead to states of unrest.

Inequality in appointments and promotion and selection of incompetent people had breed mediocrity in the rank of the workforce. This is a problem sown by the government and the leadership class.

To further on Ben Carson's statement, in my own words: It is politicians that escalate prejudices to divide and rule the people. Many of the 21st century religious and tribal clashes often have the involvement of government, its leaders and politicians - many times.

It is time we wake up and realize that it was the government and politicians who created many of those problems we want them to solve.

The government cannot solve the problem it created in the first place. It takes the people to solve this and several other problems of the world.

Whatever move of enduring change must begin with the people and not the government. The best any government can do is to midwife the project, policy or program. If the individual citizens will be committed to bringing a solution to the society, it will become difficult for the government to stand on their way: for the advancing man everything else advances with him.

In view of the above, the change Nigeria needs is you. For so long you have been conditioned to think that the government or a force out there needs to be corrected before you can live that dream life of yours. To keep looking outward especially the government is to waste away and sentence your life to mediocrity. Would you agree that you are doomed just because the government had failed?

This book is written for you and many people like you to do something. What I always tell people when the government is failing in responsibility is this: the government is confuse and bereft of adequate knowledge to move forward. In actual fact, the government is looking for that man with the right answer. You should choose to be the man.

The failure of the government is your own opportunity to be

showcased. If you possess the solution and means to assist people around, they will seek you and the government will court you.

To complain is to be frustrated and to murmur is to surrender. Tell yourself, I know what to do. Don't go down the drain where the multitude end up, waiting for a handout from the little god called government.

You are created by God with an immense capability to create your world to suit your dream. If you believe, no government can reduce you or limit how far you can go, reach or aspire to be. The world is your oyster, we are in a global community, which imperatively means that you cannot be limited except by forces you submit to; men in the 21st Century are doing things beyond the border of their nations.

Whatever type of government you may have around you, see it as an opportunity. The more deplorable the situation is, the more the opportunity to plant a new system. The bane of change is that we are often too quick to join the bandwagon.

The bandwagon keeps the deplorable condition on. People join the bandwagon because they refuse to pay the price of change which requires commitment, perseverance and hard work.

Whosoever pays the price becomes the change Nigeria needs!

I AM THE CHANGE

In the course of creating this design, I adopted this slogan "I am the change Nigeria needs". In no time it became acceptable in the communities and groups where it was shared.

The concept is to help everyone to see himself as the change Nigeria needs; and as a deviation from the old system of looking outward to the government, corporate systems and organizations we belong.

This concept does not make any attempt to look down on any form of constituted authority; instead, it is designed to empower individuals to become responsible and contributors to the development and growth of the government and world around them.

As long as we think of the need for others to change and not us, we may not have an enduring change. But when you change, everything else advances in that proportion.

The best form of change is the one that begins with you. Take this illustration very seriously and you will see the need to become the pioneer of desirable change in your world. Which one would you prefer: to be rich yourself (your own change of financial status), or to be content having someone else be rich and giving you stipends from time to time? I would rather be rich myself than wait to receive welfare package.

If you wait for someone else's change to rub off on you, you may have to wait indefinitely or settle for a token of welfare package. Some people have waited indefinitely for some false government promises that never came to be while some have lived miserable life of lack and not-enough because they put their hope on a giddy government or politicians.

Live your life as if government would fail, and it would fail sometime. The essence is that whatever happens, you would be satisfied that you lived your life to the fullest. Do not put your financial eggs in the government's basket; ask the pensioners. Don't expect the subsidy to continue, don't expect they will build that community road, and don't expect much from the government. Instead, expect much from yourself; work hard, contribute more and live to the fullest; let this be your pursuit and you will not be surprised wherever the government tilt to. If you keep building up yourself, opportunity will show forth to be the needed hands in governance and the society; and if you have laboured and become the best you can be, on the way you should have become beneficial to the world around you.

In being the change, your world will also change. This is our concept of sustainable change.

I am the change, you are the change.

The government, society and organizations are faceless, it is you and I that have faces and from each other we should expect changes. If we would not change as individual citizens, we shall not expect the nation to rise above its present decay.

What do you think you can do to add to the flavor of a sustainable change? It is time you look beyond the government. If the government could do it alone, we would long have been settled in a prosperous land with all that God bestowed us with. If the government had done it, we would not be extending the clarion call to you. The failures of government necessitated the vital call to you to become the change.

You may not have to do something big. For instance, I am not doing something unusually big at my own end. I move around, speak to leaders and individuals to brace up because they are the change. I picked my pen and write to motivate you to do all that you can. Above all, I make a pledge to become a change model and a worthy national example.

Change is the common denominator that runs through the universe, so it is a natural part of life. The only difference is that man has a will, so he must decide and choose to change in order to have his lofty dreams realized; conversely if man refuses to change by active design an adverse external change will impact on him. If you don't choose your own change process deliberately, change will be forced upon you. Forced change often carries with it negative implications. Choose to make changes deliberately, for change is in everyone's nature.

Choose to begin that move of a bigger and lofty life that will be a benefit to the world.

What Can You Do?

What can you do to make your service one of honour? Whatever your occupation, venture or day-to-day undertakings, take the path of honour. Be the model of change and become the hallmark of excellence.

Bear upon you the mark of distinction that separates you out from the run-of-the-mill, the ragtag and the ordinary fellow in the system. Magnify your office, vocation and job and begin to do things with self-esteem.

You are the change, if you think you are. There is a way a messenger will comport himself that he will become a lesson to be emulated by his master. One could be highly placed and yet have the personality of scoundrel and the low life.

On the other side, one could be lowly placed and possess the personality of kings. After all, what we are on the inside is more important than what we are on the outside.

Jose Alberto Mujica, the president of Uruguay was known for a simple lifestyle. He drives an old beetle Volkswagen and without the usual entourage and pomp that follows other world leaders; yet he remains a respected world leader compared to many buccaneers who occupy leadership offices in Africa.

There is a quote alluded to him: "I am called 'the poorest president', but I don't feel poor". He added: "A poor person is not someone who has little but one who needs infinitely more, and more and more. I don't live in poverty, I live in simplicity".

Poverty of the mind is the worst disease anyone could be infected with. It takes away rest from a man and makes him to struggle to grab all through his life. Poverty of the mind makes a man to always want more of anything the heart seek after without decency or decorum.

Poverty is a feeling; more money does not make you feel rich. I have seen people with barely enough who have a look of being rich because they are contented while some have more money yet look mean and crude in their pursuit of more; because of greed such people, in order to satisfy their greed lose their joy and destroy everything on their way.

Does it worth it to take away the happiness of others, steal community owned resources, maim and kill for our own comfort?

Does it worth it to slander and smear other people's reputation in the soil because of politics, power, fame, prominence and position? Does it worth it to lose our self-respect, dignity and self-esteem because of greed? What honour is left for our office when we use it primarily as an avenue to take advantage over others?

The change we need is the one that creates more life for everybody; agitation for personal reasons and enrichment cannot be sustained for long because at the end it makes everything small and destroy everything in its trail. Sustainable change is an all-inclusive thing. This is why terrorism and militancy will never give birth to a beautiful life, the means employed to achieve a goal will tell you the end of it.

Those who employ crude means to achieve their end desires destroy themselves along the way. No matter how much money a greedy man steals he does not have the joy of possessing it in spite of his many toys. The feeling of contentment is greater than owning a bulwark of silver or bullion of gold.

No man who lived for things and selfish reasons ever find purpose; he abuses everything committed into his hands. To find contentment is to find reasons and purpose for living; when you cease living for things you begin to live for people and in the final analysis, the man who lived for people is richer in the true sense of it, more honourable and dignified. A contented man has a name but a raving greedy person has no self-esteem or honour; he lives like a brutish beast driven by his appetite without reason or understanding.

The man who lives for himself is pretty small and has no memorial to his honour. The best he is remembered for is how he created pains in his drive for gain. The change you want for yourself should be the change you want for others.

Change begins when you are contented, and in contentment you have something to share and give irrespective of your state in life.

Change begins when a waiter knows he can give a beautiful smile without expecting anything in return.

Change begins when the law enforcement agents do not take

advantage of erring citizens to enrich themselves but instead help the citizens to abide by the law for the greater good of all. Change begins when teachers see their job as a means to build the future, mould characters and become models for their students. Change begins when they see their job beyond the pay cheque.

Change begins when the religious leaders and the followers use their creeds and beliefs to exemplify uprightness, sacrifice, honesty and true giving so that through their lifestyles people may see the worthiness of their religion. Change is when religions are used as tools to build societies and nations.

Change begins when leadership is seen as an opportunity to empower and give direction to the followers in order that the followers may maximize and realize their noblest dreams.

Change begins when politicians see their positions as a trust from the people by which to govern and inherently important they use the common resources to develop and build infrastructures, create opportunities and environment conducive for the common good. Change is when politicians see themselves as the fair umpire serving all and sundry.

Change begins when the individual is dedicated to developing himself to the fullest, acquire as much as he can materially and intellectually, possess the best tools possible and choose or find his most desired vocation, and then channel everything he has to make life better for all. As I write this paragraph, I have the example of Microsoft owner Bill Gates in mind who created a world class solution in personal computer. His solution made him the richest man in the world; with his wealth he has created one of the greatest interventions through Bill and Melinda Gates Foundation, for the disadvantaged around the world; especially Africa.

Before closing this chapter, I will present quotations of the world renowned sage, Mahatma Gandhi: Be the change you wish to see in the world.

Chapter Ten

THE ORGANIZED CHANGE

As beautiful as it is to create individual and personal change, we need to understand that man advances his activities and thrive better through organized community. Thus, we should understand that change cannot be carried out on solo mode, we need to leverage with existing platforms of organizations, corporations, sectors, and communities.

To effectively change a society, the individual change leaders have to partner with other individuals in existing platforms; raise new change leaders within the ORGANIZED platforms, these ones also go ahead to raise like-minded people who affect the rest of the world around them towards achieving the new course of change.

The effective way to achieve the change we want is when we mutually decide to change through old or new organized platforms. Nigeria as a nation cannot fare better until the people in it decide for a change. No leader can make a change or successfully impose a change except he is able to reach the heart of the people. For the fact that the society is stratified into sectors, units and organizations, a change leader will get through much easily by these organized settings. This is a pointer to the fact that a leader will successfully create the change he wants when he has people aligned to his disposition through transformed minds.

Transform the people and you end up transforming the society: this is the sure and sustainable path. There are two case studies of wrong ways of effecting change; one was at the federal level while the other was at the state level. Not too long ago, the federal government felt the need to remove subsidy from petrol. The need arose as a result of diversionary acts of some cabals who render the subsidy program non-rewarding to national cause.

The large scale diversion and fraud involved made it worthwhile to remove the subsidy, although it was a good idea but the citizens especially the illiterates, low income earners and the ignorant citizens found it difficult to understand. The previous administration attempt met with great protests that nearly tore the country apart. The next administration finally succeeded through a somewhat imposition despite agitations.

My personal view is that there is a better way through organized consultation using facts and figures. The government should be able to illustrate in pictures where we were, the losses incurred and the ultimate negative outcomes and the same time give us lucid picture of incremental growth achievable when the subsidy is removed.

Government should begin to find ways to sell herself to her citizens the same way a businessman would sell a deal; possibly enhance this through graphical illustrations. When the common man on the street fails to understand a government program, he tends to see it as government thing even when the benefits are targeted toward the welfare of the masses.

A good way to start is the government presenting the new concept to diverse organized group leaders for onward communication to their subjects on the need arising. If the government makes a good presentation, there wouldn't be much outrage when the change is made.

If you will observe, this follows the same formula governments adopt to spread their propaganda, the difference is instead of selling propaganda, the government is actually delivering a sincere, laudable and inclusive positive change agenda.

A child will bear the hunger when he is sure that the food on fire is for him. When the citizens are sure of the sincerity of the government regarding their welfare, they will endure longer.

To coax, intimidate or force a program on the people is the lazy approach by leaders. It does not create lasting change of the realm. This is the very reason why program sustainability is difficult in this part of the world. Unfortunately, the government has always believed it has the power to do anything; so doing without consultation or interaction of any kind with the citizens. Communication breeds trust, lack of it creates animosity and ill feelings.

The second example of poor transformation project was at the state level. A governor wanted to run a Public-Private Partnership on some secondary schools. Instead of consulting with relevant stakeholders he went directly to the media to announce his intention. This led to much tension which nearly got out of hands. Stakeholders in the religious sectors, labour groups, human rights activists, parents, teachers and students ganged up to fight the intention. They were not well informed about the benefits, so the governor's good intention was misconstrued while the opposition group used it as an opportunity to attack this laudable idea (it turned out finally to be laudable).

A government could have a good change program that could benefit individual citizens yet find it difficult to sell it out, if he failed to carry along the relevant organized sectors, he may meet with brick walls. Many times, to reach the individual citizens you will need to pass through the organized sectors.

People tend to trust the words of their leaders and that of people around them than what the media would do. The media is a good tool for outreaching but should be applied after the in-reach consultations with relevant stakeholders. Anytime and any day, the word-of-mouth approach to getting result is more powerful than the influence of the media. Leaders and personalities are endowed with power-of-mouth and just the right word is capable of giving endorsement to a project of change.

Some of the notable organized sectors that can be found within the society include:

The Traditional Bodies

This includes the traditional heads, their chiefs and the subjects. In Africa, we still have much attachment to our tradition and the custodians of such in every community. This bond makes it easy to integrate traditional leaders as veritable stakeholders in communicating with the citizens.

The Labour Groups

Labour Groups and associations would continue to wax stronger by the day as they continue to stand to protect the interests of members; in return members would give their loyalty to the cause their leaders believe in. The Labour Groups and associations are very large; their supports for any cause can make so much difference.

The Nigerian Labour Union (Congress) is a big umbrella which is multi-sectored in a sense because it covers Labour Groups from the private sectors to the public sectors; the health, engineering, manufacturing, media, and many others. The body has the capability to help catalyzed a project in their own way.

The Religious Group

Personally, I see religious groups and organizations as powerful agents of change when coordinated to achieve this. The one big clause is that most religions don't see their responsibilities towards the community, state and the nation. The members who are citizens often hold the parochial stand for only a cause relating to their devised faith and shun the real faith which covers social responsibilities and support to societal development.

But if religions leaders would for once move away from selfish entanglement and direct their members to serve the world, things will get better and the nation will witness drastic change and advancement.

The Private Sectors

This is another notable group. It is the engine room of enterprise development and economic growth. To get this group involved would definitely make much difference because this sector constitutes the economy hub: a government policy or project can be grounded if the support of the private sector is not sought. For within the private sector we have large multinationals that employ thousands of employees who are citizens and within it are large organizations and rich owners whose sponsorship, funding or influence would be required from time to time.

Again, they need to be well consulted because any adversarial policy or change project may lead to capital flight or behind door anti-policy propaganda through their sponsorship.

The Entertainment Group

The entertainment platforms which comprises of showbiz, music and sports are very powerful tools to engage and a good access to get across to the citizens. The roles of celebrities and sport stars to engage and influence citizens cannot be over-emphasized; a single celebrity could have influence on as much as a million followers. Consider the leveraging potentials, and the ease of communication between a celebrity and the followers.

The above sectors and groups are few among the organized platforms one can leverage on in order to amplify a change project. By involving the leaders one can reach out to the teaming citizens under them within a very short time.

Core Area

At the end of the day, we hope to draw out change leaders from these major bodies: religion and the social sectors, private, education, political and government, sports, media and entertainment sectors.

To have a well rounded and sustainable change, all sectors have to be involved and reached out to. A one sided re-branding or change project can never be effective.

The core areas where I feel change leaders are needed include: the religious groups and organizations, civil service, police, schools, transport, market people and artisans, farmers, armed forces, health and others.

The ultimate purpose for reaching out to all sectors is to emphasize and transplant into the citizens a new culture that embrace positive values geared towards participatory development as each of us become the vital change!

Some Area Where Change is Expedient

1. National Values.

The value a nation holds unto will determine the height a nation can ever rise to. Does a nation reward excellence or mediocrity? Do we give honour and recognition to the competent, hard working Nigerian or we have other ulterior measuring stick that present inequalities?

Honesty, fairness, equity, and equality should reflect in our national values, and showcased as our national brand. These values should be woven into the fabrics of every sector.

2. Performance and Service Delivery

Change should be brought to bear on increasing the performance of the Nigerian workforce through a new culture of industry. This is also intended to bear on improving on quality, creativity and innovation.

Economic growth cannot rest on the shoulder of mediocrity. The economic outlook of any society is dependent on the workforce; therefore, change cannot be sustained without improving on the quality of work input and output; and the culture of innovation needs to be impressed because this will propel the development of exportable goods and services. Through this we can rise to become the center of international trades.

3. Management and Leadership

The government is the primary manager of our national resources. We need such reform whereby resources are appropriately channeled and distributed in a way that it reflects growth and development. As managers, resources are expected to be put into effective use in a way that it will profit every citizen equitably.

Those who assume the position of managers should understand their positions as custodians and not destroyer of the common good. Reformation in management means control and monitoring of resources towards making everyone's life better.

Managers of resources outside the government purview also need reformation in order to check-mate the effect of corruption that has stained every segment of the society.

Leadership Reform is also required. This starts with recruitment and appointment of the right people to do the job; raising leaders who will offer the nation blueprints and directions that will translate towards progress and development.

4. Local Production

No nation can move forward if the bulk of her people are tilted toward consumerism. Since the discovery of oil, entrepreneurship and local content development has tilted downward.

Nigeria is known as the hub of raw materials to the international market some decades ago. Our local production of raw materials such as cocoa, groundnut and palm oil was enlarged some decades back but we are presently near zero. We have become so lazy that we began to import the food we eat! This is damnable and terribly bad.

If we cannot feed ourselves, how do we expand on entrepreneurship? No change can be sustained when a people cannot independently feed itself and when there is no enterprise growth. For without local content production and enterprise growth, an economy will continue to be on the deficit.

Change should include the ability to feed ourselves, maximize on the extractive industries and creating an environment conducive for enterprise development; empowering more citizens to become entrepreneurs and employers of labour.

Goals to Sustainable Change

Whatever we do, there should be an underlying goal or objective. This is what makes the effort worthwhile.

1. One of the goals we should strive to achieve in realizing a sustainable change is to correct the vicious cycle of underdevelopment through a new set of rule; learning to do things differently by welcoming models that support advancement from any part of the world and ready to jettison whatever is not working that were established through sentiments.

Principles don't fail. Looking intently, the developed nations often have similar principles that guide their existence and operations. If we really want to advance, we must learn and adopt such principles and ideologies.

Remember, nothing founded on sentiments lasts long, but principles abides. It's time we took up new rules of engagement set on abiding principles, frameworks and models. For instance, if India gets it right in the area of medicine and manufacturing, wisdom demands that we learn from them in those areas. If American federal system of government is superior in certain sense, it is wisdom to learn the certain ideology to replace the ideologies of federation we have erroneously over time built on sentiments.

2. The second important goal is to breed competent change leaders in all sectors who will drive the empowerment and participation of citizens. The concept of sustainable change is based firstly on empowerment of followers, looking out for their welfare, making their lives better and giving them room to participate amply in the achievement of the set vision. The leader should always be aware that

the change he achieved alone can never be sustained; continuity requires that we act as a collective entity. Without competent leaders there will not be drivers to push through a change process.

3. Another goal is to connect with others. The change we need is expected to help raise patriotic citizens and nationalist; people who put national cause above personal, tribal or religions sentiment; being interested in the bigger cause of humanity and having the knowledge that service to humanity is service to God as we work together to create abundance and prosperity for all .

When a citizen is concerned about the next citizen, we will grow into a better society but when citizens care only for their own cause at the expense of others, we end up raising a community of grabbers; this will cause a nation to regress into a state of anarchy. In this, we should understand that making the next person better is an indirect way of helping ourselves to get better. If you promote peace, you will live in a peaceful home, society and nation. Your world is a reflection of you. To connect with others is to build-in the capability to sustain what you have at hand.

4. One other big goal is to identify great values necessary for building an emerging society; and making it the denominator of our daily transactions. If everybody begins to talk about honesty and our actions are weighed and rewarded accordingly upon the balance of honesty, then honesty will thrive.

We cannot become what we scarcely think or talk about. Values grow in proportion to how much we think, ponder and talk about it; it takes roots when actions are weighed upon it. We cannot talk, extol and encourage vices and expect good values to be promoted. Again, vices such as indolence, corruption and malpractice festers when it is rewarded or encouraged.

We should bear it in mind that a nation will fall or rise by the yardstick of the value it tolerates. Transformation of any society has a strong correlation with the values they promote. Therefore, to build a sustainable change, we need to begin the promotion of new value system that go with the kind of change we want; if only we do not pay mere lips service to it. Thus, our commitment to new set of values would be the real indicator that we are set for a change.

5. The final goal in my list is to give relevance to every citizen. Make the ordinary man on the street feel important; appreciating their roles and giving them recognition through diverse agencies and organized platforms. The way to do this is giving them opportunity to participate in achieving goals that have direct impact and benefit to them. Participation and engagement give one the sense of ownership.

Denominator to Change

There are factors that drive changes and make it easy to attain:

1. Foremost is the spread of the right kind of knowledge or information. An idea or policy may sound good, but if the citizens lack adequate knowledge of it, it may not sail through.

Citizens need adequate knowledge about national programs; this will further help in mobilizing them to participate in sustaining such programs. Scanty knowledge breeds apathetic supporters. More so, the wrong kind of knowledge will often drift citizens to follow after programs inimical to their welfare. For instance, the wrong knowledge that national cake is to be shared will lead a nation down the hill.

Having a laudable program does not translate that the citizens would know except you communicate it. To know is to communicate, share and to explain until a mutual drive is achieved. Sustained change requires mutual drive because it must involve citizens' participation. Adequate knowledge sharing between the leader and the followers is the bedrock of sustainable development and growth.

2. Real change requires sacrifice; nothing great is achieved with ease. We cannot continue in self indulgence and automatically come up successful in life. A government that is not frugal in spending on subsidy, social welfare and remunerations will have little left for developmental purpose. A healthy economy is more than sharing pecks and welfare packages: It is fundamentally about development

and growth.

The above statements may not make senses to the common and average person on the street. Let us look at it closely: when a society is in its highly developed state, the infrastructure being in place, the environment conducive for economic growth, wealth creation, enterprise development and employment, the people will hardly seek for social welfare package.

Self indulgence whether of individual, corporate bodies or public service does not support development. On this premise, the spirit of sacrifice and patriotism should be promoted by the leaders. More so, it should be seen in their personal lives and inculcated as a lifestyle into the citizens. Sacrifice is an important driver of change.

3. Real change requires contributions from every quarter. There should be obligatory demand on all regions, tiers of governments and communities. All sectors and citizens should be expected to come up with a personal or group project or program towards nation building. And in fairness, recognition and more rewards should go to those who contribute more.

I think the new shift towards real growth should be based on equitable resource sharing reflecting on contribution, performance, ability and value given. To share resources based on population size, religious balance and ethnic bases may not give room for competitive growth.

Just as you cannot successfully fly a plane on one wing, so you cannot sustain a change from imbalance or one-sided contribution. You cannot drive a national change project through one tribe, religious set up, parochial sentiments, repression or cheating on one group in favour of another. Remember, the nation belongs to all and has to be sustained through the supports of all.

4. There must be synergy and cohesive bond within the system if things must work. It is possible to make sacrifice to a cause without any connection and to make contribution without synergy. The bonding is what makes the people to work together without ill feelings or sentiments. The bond creates the staying power until

things work out, and it is what finally makes the sacrifice and contributions to become profitable.

It is the bond that makes the diverse tribal and ethnic groups to forge ahead in spite of differences; this is what helps to align the diverse religions to the benefit of the nation and citizens.

Synergy is what brings together the beauty of diversity, differences of classes and status to create more strength for all. Synergy makes each unit stronger therefore true change should allow for synergy and invariably bring benefits to all.

5. There must be cultivation of the spirit of self-dependence. Individual should see himself empowered to effect and make positive changes without necessarily having to wait for any godfather or the government. Self dependence is the ability to forge ahead without restrains and create alternative pathways to achieve ones aims in life. When you are self dependent you are no longer one of the problems, a source of concern to be pitied in the society. A self dependent man is a solution provider.

The average citizen could choose to wait for measly help and largesse from government but not you. Instead of adding to the number of unemployed, you ought to come out among them as you create or generate your own job and for others.

Self dependent citizens believe in their inherent capabilities to chart their own course even in the face of dire leadership mismanagement and abuse.

6. A debtor is a slave to his creditor and a beggar is a servant to his benefactor. A nation cannot sustain a change without economic power. Lack of sustenance creates internal crisis in our respective homes, so it affects the nation at large. The international big players know how to play world politics with nations that have weak economy and are rendered perpetually as slaves.

A self sustained economy means a nation can meet up with or be supplied with their own basic needs without external aids. A nation on the path of transformation should make it a strong cardinal to work out means to become self sustained especially of basic needs: food, shelter, and clothing along with social amenities; without being into economic bondage of the stronger economy in the world. In the journey to economic prominence, you cannot grow at pal with another nation to which you are indebted.

7. Finally, our individual commitment to national interest is vital to the evolution of a great nation and economy. The nation's interest is all inclusive activities that pursue the interests of her citizens in terms of activities, programs and projects that are beneficiary and with an end result of making life better for all.

When personal interests are championed on a large scale above that of the state, such a society will remain perpetually backward. When religion or tribal interests becomes tool to sabotage the common good of the citizens then no change or development can actually be achieved.

The Roles of the Organized Sectors Leaders

Leaders who truly seek for sustainable changes whether in the society or corporate world have to follow the model in this book by starting with development and empowerment of their followers as a matter of urgency.

Making money or harnessing the resources or opportunity around them should become a secondary drive. Change leaders in corporate world should be people-focused; having interests in the welfare and development of their followers. Thus, the corporation that wants to become sustained should be concerned about solutions and benefits it has to offer to clients and workers while income should become a derivative. An organization that puts the welfare of its people above all else will have people around her for a longer time and with people comes wealth creation. No wealth creation without people.

Develop your people and they will in turn develop your organization. Build around yourself alone and soon you will have what you build collapse before your very eye. You need people to sustain what you started whether business, project or organization. These people need to be empowered in order to take your organization to the next level.

You cannot afford to keep dwarfs around you because of fear or selfishness. By building leaders and empowering others you become leader of leaders.

No matter what your business or organization is into, if it is purposed for the good of humanity, it should afford everyone that comes around it to be more than they were when they initially teamed up with you. It should serve as an empowerment platform for everyone who wished to be developed.

Let every organization move away from the barbaric and archaic corporate thinking where employees, clients, members and followers are seen as mere tools to enlarge their greed.

The 21st Century emerging thought for organization is to take up the responsibility to become the value centered organization; giving out more and empowering everyone that is connected to the organization.

If every organization whether profit or non-profit becomes compliant to the concept of sustainable change through empowerment of individual to lead a degree of change in the organization and the society, the nation will begin her way to greatness.

Let every leader help his followers to see themselves as the change needed to move the organization upward and not just a mere tool to be used and dumped. Let them see each other as vitally important for the upward transformation of their organization and nation. Remember, leaders have the power of influence to mar or make their followers.

EPILOGUE

The Crux

Citizens' empowerment and participation is crucial to national and world transformation. The best of leaders are those who empower and engage their followers and members. The new concept of change should require each member, citizen or sector to contribute to the development and execution of policies, programs and activities at hand.

As we come to the close of this book, leaders should drop the idea that they have all it takes as the leaders to command change through the ranks of their followers. Everybody and group have certain unique elements to inject into the whole if given a place in the big picture. Let nobody thinks that he can change the world alone without the help of others.

Again, we should be reminded that not just any person can change the world but the empowered man. In as much as you would need the people around you to support a cause, they must be excited and empowered to do so. True leadership is to take the people along and not commandeer them as puppets.

The bottom line: Nation building is every citizen's project; that is, everybody should be carried along in policy formulation and execution. Nation building is a project of all and for all citizens… but it starts with you.

You are the change!

IT IS POSSIBLE

For the South African, they held on to their dream and vision and all doggedness that apartheid has to be destroyed. Even under the apartheid regimes they never failed in reminding themselves that their dream was possible. Then, they had visionary leaders like Desmond Tutu and Nelson Mandela who empowered and motivated the people until their dream of an emancipated South African nation was realized.

Ours is not apartheid or a racial subjugation in any form; here it is our people who live to oppress one another which in my opinion is far worse. It is not much about a class or caste problem but an ideological or cultural problem whereby those who emerge up there take it all; the winner takes it all syndromes. Once we scramble to get to the top, we forget where we come from. There is an unfortunate divide between the leader and the citizens. In Nigeria, the leaders don't often see themselves as one with the people. This selfish frame has removed the link, so the rich and leaders create their own world which is in isolation and away from the common man.

This is not going to last. When the rich and the poor cannot connect, a time will come when the overwhelming difference will create a catastrophic eruption, a revolution of some sort, even anarchy; the ramifications are diverse. But we can save the situation by melting this divide now as the rich and powerful begin to build bridges of amenities, comfort, wealth and provision for the citizens. This bridge is the only way of sustaining both ends harmoniously.

It is possible to have the people-leader emerge to lead the nation into economic growth without resorting to self-enrichment. Whatever we could imagine as constituting freedom for every citizen as we have in the advance nation is possible here. This belief of possibility underlies the basis of sustainable change we so much desire as a nation.

When we begin to hope for possibilities, then the system will begin to form towards the realization of credible leaders. The hope of possibility is an empowering state that makes us fully aware that we are the architect and the maker of the world we live in, meaning that we have a positive part to play. Great leadership is possible.

We should believe that Nigerian politics will not always be controlled by money and the highest bidder. With hope and faith, the value system will begin to shift as we raise men and women who are not swayed by money or fame and without being influenced by subtle interests against the common good.

With hope we can have a strong system that produces exceptional candidates through free, fair and credible electoral process. We can believe in the possibility of having free and fair elections where leaders are produced without vested interest than needful for national cause.

It is no longer a hidden fact that the crafty ones hold sway in Nigeria's leadership terrain till this moment and many are not intellectually fit to create the wonders as required of a 21st century society. Many of their acts are not different from what their fore-fathers did by selling their subjects into slavery for cheap perishables like mirrors, gunpowder, gins and clothes; it is possible to learn from history and not repeat the inglorious history of shame.

If we will all think deeply and mend the fence on our sides we will soon begin to run a society built on leadership by merit; reconstruct of government of merit and people of merit; meritocracy instead of the lopsided democracy that has not helped the nation one bit. The government of the people should be one run on merit towards the uplifting of the people.

I have a dream that one day in no distant future those who merit leadership roles will be put ahead of diverse sentiments; those who are fit will be sought after to help fix the mess of poor leadership so long entrenched. I hope that when that time comes, you will support the birth of merit and be one of the competent ones to yield the nation on the path of meaning. I believe that very soon Nigeria will line up in her leadership train great technocrats, think tanks, experts and gurus in various fields that would help put Nigeria in the front as a global force to be reckoned with. Then the weak and unintelligent avarice would have gone, buried deep down memory lane as we have the birth of a new and great nation; this is possible.

Through credible leadership, it is possible to have all the seemingly impossible things of today: infrastructures, quality education, food, housing, employment and all-sector round development. It is possible.

On this note, I will say: do not despair, do not give up, let us hold our hands strong and tell everybody who cares: the good life is possible here in Nigeria. Then we would have no need to rush out of our native land because instead of an exodus out of here we would have people thronging in from all corners of the world as the new found land.

It is possible.

THE ETERNAL PLACE OF POWER

The earth and the entire universe is never an accident, everything came into being by the eternal power of someone greater than us. And this greater being is God. God has interest in governance and the leadership of his people; therefore, he wants us to be concerned about those we choose to run the affairs of our lives. He is a God of purpose and his purpose in governance is to lead the people to a higher state of being; advancing the people in every facet of life; morally, technologically, educationally, and so on and so forth.

God needs good leaders even as these leaders have need of God; this is the union necessary to make the earth a better place. God would not come down to do what he has enabled men to do; at the same time man cannot work in isolation without God. This is why God is counting on credible leaders who have the mind of God and the mind of the people they set to lead. A good leader in spite of his natural competence will always seek for what is pleasing to God and by all duty of honesty stand to execute such; choosing in this token to uphold the universal values of goodness, love, peace, honesty, equity and unity upon which godliness is established.

Leaders will always get to the point where their natural strength and wisdom will fail them such as we have seen during recessions, natural disasters, wars, human disillusionment and other moments as such. There are moments the leader would be down and weep like a baby; when no human aid could sustain him. The leader of people must be able to count on supernatural support at all times, especially in such times of crises.

Thus, those who will lead the people should be leaders that know God and his will of goodness and abundance for his people; composed in making the lives of the subjects better. We need leaders who will lead us as a people to our promised land of a better and fulfilling living. This would be a leader of a kind that has access to God's power to change the world for better, leading an extraordinary impact on the world as he has his name etched on the marble of time and times.

No leader makes any meaningful impact through self indulgence, selfish pursuit and personal moral standing. The strength of every true leader of people in all ages originates basically from God and hinges on the spiritual awareness of this source and built upon the foundation of selflessness, truth, love and peace in his entire realm. No leader can live in this higher estate of love, peace, truth and selflessness without the knowledge of God, the creator of all beings. Man by innate drive is greedy, selfish and riotous, thus it takes a relationship with a spiritual God to transcend the lower estate of man.

God-factor makes the difference whether a leader will make good delivery to his people or not. Consider the elder statesmen of America during their independence era. They offer with all boldness and affirmation ideologies and constitution built on the knowledge of The Eminent God; we have among the early leaders of America God fearing men like George Washington, and Thomas Jefferson: the foundation they gave to this nation testifies to the need to have leaders who know God in this part of the world; and are not shy of the fact of relating with the Living God. America most noted leader, President Abraham Lincoln was a man that has led his nation in many public prayers to our God and creator in their moment of crises. He was never shy of the great help that comes to rulers of people that trust and walk with God.

If Nigeria will ever sigh for relief from corrupt and wicked leaders, the people must begin to seek for leaders who have relationship with God. To say that governance, politics and leadership belongs to cultists and godless people is to say evil should continue in our realm; God forbid. We are also not talking about having professing religionists but people who have histories backed up with moral standing, worthy lifestyles and amiable personality that radiate the essence of godliness. The fact that someone pays huge sum to defray religious activities doesn't mean he has the knowledge of God; he may be one of those who seek cheap popularity through the religious divides. Seeking for prayers to perpetuate self in power does not signify a love and relationship with God.

The leader that loves God must love the people. God created and seek for the advancement of his subjects.

The leader of the people who wish to make marks on the eternal sand of history must run his affairs with the support of the Eternal God.

This is the wisdom of God

THE GAME CHANGER FOR NATIONAL TRANSFORMATION

The Real Change Nigeria Needs

Wale Adewumi presents a compelling anatomy of bottom-up change as panacea for national transformation, creating a paradigm shift towards governance and effective ideological transfer.

It is a book for those who want to grow in influence, create a boomerang and sustain the tempo of transformation in an amazing way. This is a magnificent glimpse into the secrets of generational icons. Follow through, be transformed and get set to transform the next generation.

Wale goes beyond repeating the old fad that does not work.

Warning: Reading this book will change you!

WALE ADEWUMI passion for nation building project has spanned about two decades. He has pioneered many campaigns and speaking engagements. He is a social entrepreneur, consultant, speaker and prolific writer with more than 20 books (published and unpublished scripts) to his name.

www.ingramcontent.com/pod-product-compliance
Lightning Source LLC
Chambersburg PA
CBHW051310250726
48656CB00004B/1584